Allyn & Bacon
Casebook Series
Domestic Violence

Edited by

Jerry L. Johnson

Grand Valley State University

George Grant, Jr.

Grand Valley State University

PEARSON

Boston   New York   San Francisco
Mexico City   Montreal   Toronto   London   Madrid   Munich   Paris
Hong Kong   Singapore   Tokyo   Cape Town   Sydney

To all of those who have helped, advised, supported, criticized,
and forgiven. You know who you are.
Jerry L. Johnson

To my wife, Beverly, who inspires and supports me
in all my endeavors. In loving memory of my father and mother,
George and Dorothy Grant.
George Grant, Jr.

Series Editor: *Patricia Quinlin*
Marketing Manager: *Kris Ellis-Levy*
Production Administrator: *Janet Domingo*
Compositor: *Galley Graphics*
Composition Buyer: *Linda Cox*
Manufacturing Buyer: *JoAnne Sweeney*
Cover Coordinator: *Rebecca Krzyzaniak*

For related titles and support materials, visit our online catalog at www.ablongman.com.

Library of Congress Cataloging-in-Publication Data

Allyn & Bacon casebook series for domestic violence / edited by Jerry L. Johnson, George
Grant, Jr.—1st ed.
    p. cm.
    Includes bibliographical references.
    ISBN 0-205-38952-X (pbk.)
    1. Abused women—Case studies.   2. Victims of family violence—Case studies.   3. Social
work with women—Case studies.   4. Family violence—Case studies.   I. Title: Allyn and
Bacon casebook series for domestic violence.   II. Johnson, Jerry L.   III. Grant,
George, Jr.
HV1444.A56 2005
362.82′92—dc22

                                                                                    2004052966

Printed in the United States of America

10 9 8 7 6 5 4 3 2   09 08 07 06 05

Contents

Preface   v

1 *A Multi-Systemic Approach to Practice*   1
Jerry L. Johnson & George Grant, Jr.

2 *Mikki's Story*   29
Carolyn Jumpper-Black & Sandra Shelly

3 *Betty and Charlie Bristol*   69
Shelley Schuurman

4 *Faith Harper*   93
Kim Wetterman & Heidi Weipert

Preface

This text offers students the chance to study the work of experienced social workers practicing with domestic violence cases. As graduate and undergraduate social work educators, we (the editors) have struggled to find quality practice materials that translate well into a classroom setting. Over the years, we have used case materials from our practice careers, professionally produced audiovisuals, and tried other casebooks. While each had its advantages, we could not find a vehicle that allowed students to study the work of experienced practitioners that took students beyond the belief that practice is a technical endeavor that involves finding "correct" interventions to solve client problems.

We want our students to study and analyze how experienced practitioners think about practice and how they struggle to resolve ethical dilemmas and make treatment decisions that meet the needs of their clientele. We want students to review and challenge the work of others in a way that allows them to understand what comprises important practice decisions with real clients in real practice settings. That is, we want classroom materials that allow students entry into the minds of experienced practitioners.

Goals of the Casebook

This Casebook focuses on practice with domestic violence clients in a variety of settings and from diverse backgrounds. Our goal is to provide students with an experience that:

1. Provides personal and intimate glimpses into the thinking and actions of experienced practitioners as they work with clients. In each case, students may demonstrate their understanding of the cases and how and/or why the authors approached their case in the manner presented.

2. Provides a vehicle to evaluate the processes, ideas, and methods used by the authors. We also wanted to provide students a chance to present their ideas about how they would have worked differently with the same case.
3. Affords students the opportunity to use evidence-based practice findings (Gibbs, 2003; Cournoyer, 2004) as part of the case review and planning process. We challenge students to base practice judgments and case planning exercises on current practice evidence available through library and/or electronic searches and on practice wisdom gained through consultation and personal experience when the evidence is conflicted or lacking.

To meet our goals, the cases we included in this text focus on the practice process, specifically client engagement, assessment, and the resultant clinical process, including the inevitable ethical dilemmas that consistently arise in daily practice. We aim to demonstrate the technical and artistic elements involved in developing and managing the various simultaneous processes involved in practice. While we recognize the difficulty of presenting process information (circular) in a linear medium (book), we have tried to do the best job possible toward this end.

To achieve our goals, we include in-depth case studies in this text. In these cases, authors guide students through the complete practice process, from initial contact to client termination and practice evaluation. Focusing heavily on multi-systemic client life history (see Chapter 1), students get a detailed look into the life history and presentation of the client. Then, we challenge students to "finish the case" by using client information and classroom learning to develop a written narrative assessment, diagnostic statement, treatment and intervention plan, termination and follow-up plan, and a plan to evaluate practice. We have used these cases as in-class exercises, the basis for semester-long term papers, and as comprehensive final examinations that integrate multifaceted student learning in practice courses across the curriculum.

Rationale

As former practitioners, we chose the cases carefully. Therefore, the cases in this text focus on the process (thinking, planning, and decision-making) of social work practice and not necessarily on techniques or outcome. Do not be fooled by this statement. Obviously, we believe in successful client outcome based, at least in part, on the use of evidence-based practice methods and current research findings. As important as this is, it is not our focus here—with good reason. Our experience suggests that instructive process occurs in cases that have successful and unsuccessful outcomes. In fact, we often learned more from unsuccessful cases than successful cases. We learned the most when events did not play out as planned. While some of the cases were terminated successfully, others were not. This is not a commentary on the author or the author's skill level. Everyone has cases (sometimes too many) that do not turn out as planned. We chose cases based on one simple criterion: did it provide the best possible hope for practice education? We asked authors to teach practice by considering cases that were interesting and difficult, regardless of outcome. We did not want the Casebook to become simply a vehicle to promote practice brilliance.

Mostly, we wanted this text to differ from other casebooks, because we were unsatisfied with casebooks as teaching tools. As part of the process of planning our Casebooks, we reviewed other casebooks and discussed with our graduate and undergraduate students approaches that best facilitated learning in the classroom. We discovered that many students were also dissatisfied with a casebook approach to education, for a variety of reasons. Below, we briefly address what our students told us about casebooks in general.

1. *Linear presentation.* One of the most significant problems involves case presentation. Generally, this involves two issues: linearity and brevity. Most written case studies give students the impression that practice actually proceeds smoothly, orderly, and in a sequential manner. These cases often leave students believing—or expecting—that clinical decisions are made beforehand and that practice normally proceeds as planned. In other words, students often enter the field believing that casework follows an "*A, leads to B, leads to C, leads to clients living happily ever after*" approach.

Experienced practitioners know better. In over 40 years of combined social work practice in a variety of settings, we have learned—often the "hard way"—that the opposite is true. We rarely, if ever, had a case proceed sequentially, whether our client is an individual, couple, family, group, community, or classroom. That is, the process of engagement (including culturally competent), assessment, treatment planning, intervention, and follow-up occurs in a circular manner, rooted in the client's social, physical, and cultural context, and includes consideration of the practitioner, the organization, and the laws and policies that affect and/or determine the boundaries of social work practice and treatment funding.

Practice evolves in discontinuous cycles over time, including time-limited treatments mandated by the managed care system. Therefore, real-life clinical practice—just as in all developing human relationships—seems to consistently require making stops and starts, taking wrong-turns, and even, in some cases, having "do-overs." While the goal of competent practice is to facilitate an orderly helping process that includes planned change (Timberlake, Farber, & Sabatino, 2002), practice, as an orderly process, is more often a goal (or a myth) than planned certainty. Given the linearity of case presentations discussed above, readers are often left without an appreciation or understanding of practice as process.

Additionally, many of the case presentation texts we reviewed provided "hard" client data and asked students to develop treatment plans based on this data. Yet, as any experienced practitioner knows, the difficulty in practice occurs during engagement and data collection. The usual case approach often overlooks this important element of practice. While a book format limits process writing, we believe that the case format we devised here brings students closer to the "real thing."

2. *Little focus on client engagement.*   As we like to remind students, there are two words in the title of our profession: social and work. In order for the "work" to be successful, students must learn to master the "social"—primarily, client engagement and relationship building. Social work practice is relationship based (Saleebey, 2002) and, from our perspective, relies more on the processes involved in relationship building and client engagement than technical intervention skills (Johnson, 2004). Successful practice is often rooted more in the ability of practitioners to develop open and trusting relationships with clients than on their ability to employ specific methods of intervention (Johnson, 2004).

Yet, this critically important element of practice often goes understated or ignored. Some texts even assume that engagement skills somehow exist before learning about practice. We find this true in casebooks and primary practice texts as well. When it is discussed, engagement and relationship building are presented as technical processes that also proceed in linear fashion. Our experience with students, employees, and practitioner/trainees over the last two decades suggests that it is wrong to assume that students and/or practitioners have competent engagement or relationship-building skills. From our perspective, developing a professional relationship that involves trust and openness, where clients feel safe to dialogue about the most intimate and sometimes embarrassing events in their lives, is the primary responsibility of the practitioner and often spells the difference between positive and negative client outcome (Johnson, 2004; Miller & Rollnick, 2002; Harper & Lantz, 1996). Hence, each case presentation tries to provide a sense of this difficult and often elusive process and some of the ways that the authors overcame challenges to the culturally competent client engagement process.

Target Audience

Our target audience for this text, and the others in the series, is advanced undergraduate as well as foundation and advanced graduate students in social work and other helping disciplines. We have tested our approach with students at several different points in their education. We find that the Casebooks can be used as:

- An adjunct learning tool for undergraduates preparing for or already involved in their field practicum.
- Practice education and training for foundation-level graduate students in practice theory and/or methods courses.
- An adjunct learning tool for second-year graduate students in field practicum.
- An adjunct learning tool for undergraduate and/or graduate students in any practice courses pertaining to specific populations.

While we are social work educators, we believe the Casebooks will be useful in social work and other disciplines in the human services, including counseling psychology, mental health, and specialty disciplines such as marriage and family therapy, substance abuse, and mental health degree or certificate programs. Any educational or training program designed to prepare students to work with clients in a helping capacity may find the Casebooks useful as a learning tool.

Structure of Cases

We organized the case studies to maximize critical thinking, use of professional literature, evidence-based practice knowledge, and classroom discussion in the learning process. At various points throughout each case, we comment on issues and/or dilemmas highlighted by the case. Our comments always end with a series of questions designed to focus student learning by calling on their ability to find and evaluate evidence from the professional literature and through classroom discussion. We ask students to collect evidence on different sides of an issue, evaluate that evidence, and develop a professional position that they can defend in writing and/or discussion with other students in the classroom or seminar setting.

We hope that you find the cases and our format as instructive and helpful in your courses as we have in ours. We have field-tested our format in courses at our university, finding that students respond well to the length, depth, and rigor of the case presentations. Universally, students report that the case materials were an important part of their overall learning process.

Organization of the Text

We organized this text to maximize its utility in any course. Chapter 1 provides an overview of the Advanced Multi-Systemic (AMS) practice approach. We provide this as one potential organizing tool for students to use while reading and evaluating the subsequent cases. This chapter offers students an organized and systematic framework to use when analyzing cases and/or formulating narrative assessments, treatments, and intervention plans. Our intent is to provide a helpful tool, not to make a political statement about the efficacy or popularity of one practice framework versus others. In fact, we invite faculty and students to apply whatever practice framework they wish when working with the cases.

In Chapter 2, author *Carolyn Jumpper-Black, Ph.D.,* and *Sandra Shelly, MSW.* present their work in **Mikki's Story.** Mikki was a domestic violence survivor who struggled to find her way out of a lifelong pattern of abuse by the men in her life. Jumpper-Black and Shelly also present an alternative model for working with domestic violence based on the Stages of Change model familiar to the substance abuse field of practice. They discuss the model and provide insight into its utility in practice with domestic violence.

In Chapter 3, *Shelley Schuurman, MSW, CSW,* presents a case involving a battered woman and her aggressive child in residential treatment after assaulting his teacher. In a case entitled **Charlie and Betty Bristol,** Schuurman demonstrates the difficulties involved in treating a domestic violence case and its effects on everyone in the family. Schuurman also navigates the complexities of the multi-systemic environment of professional helping systems, sometimes sending mixed messages.

The final chapter, **Faith Harper,** presents the work of *Kim Wetterman, RSW,* and *Heidi Weipert, MA, LLPC, NCC,* with a Kenyan woman trying to recover her children in a custody battle with her husband. This case has it all, domestic violence, sexual abuse, and a professional helping system that refuses to believe Faith's horrendous stories of abuse. Wetterman and Weipert present a case that demonstrates the good and bad of helping systems.

Acknowledgments

We would like to thank the contributors to this text, Carolyn Jumpper-Black, Sandra Shelly, Shelley Schuurman, Kim Wetterman, and Heidi Weipert, for their willingness to allow their work to be challenged and discussed in a public venue. We would also like to thank Patricia Quinlin and her people at Allyn and Bacon for their faith in the Casebook Series and in our ability to manage 14 manuscripts at once. Additionally, we have to thank all of our students and student assistants who served as "guinea pigs" for our case studies. Their willingness to provide honest feedback contributes mightily to this series.

Jerry L. Johnson—I want to thank my wife, Cheryl, for her support and willingness to give me the time and encouragement to write and edit. I also owe a debt of gratitude to my dear friend Hope, for being there when I need her the most.

George Grant, Jr.—I want to thank Dean Rodney Mulder and Dr. Elaine Schott for their insight, encouragement, and support during this process. I also thank Dr. Julius Franks and Professor Daniel Groce for their intellectual discourse and unwavering support.

Contributors

The Editors

Jerry L. Johnson, Ph.D., MSW, is an Associate Professor in the School of Social Work at Grand Valley State University in Grand Rapids, Michigan. He received his MSW from Grand Valley State University and his Ph.D. in Sociology from Western Michigan University. Johnson has been in social work for more than 20 years as a practitioner, supervisor, administrator, consultant, teacher, and trainer. He was the recipient of two Fulbright Scholarship awards to Albania in 1998–99 and 2000–01.

In addition to teaching and writing, Johnson serves in various consulting capacities in countries such as Albania and Armenia. He is the author of two previous books, *Crossing Borders—Confronting History: Intercultural Adjustment in a Post-Cold War World* (2000, Rowan and Littlefield) and *Fundamentals of Substance Abuse Practice* (2004, Wadsworth Brooks/Cole).

George Grant, Jr., Ph.D., MSW, is an Associate Professor in the School of Social Work at Grand Valley State University in Grand Rapids, Michigan. Grant also serves as the Director of Grand Valley State University's MSW Program. He received his MSW from Grand Valley State University and Ph.D. in Sociology from Western Michigan University. Grant has a long and distinguished career as practitioner, administrator, consultant, teacher, and trainer in social work, primarily in fields dedicated to child welfare.

Contributors

Carolyn Jumpper-Black, Ph.D., is an Associate Professor in the School of Social Work at Indiana University in Indianapolis, Indiana. Dr. Black received her MSW degree from University of Michigan in Ann Arbor, Michigan, and her Ph.D. from the University of Illinois at Chicago. Dr. Black also served as a Clinical Assistant Professor at Jane Addams College of Social Work at the University of Illinois at Chicago.

Sandra Shelly, MSW, is Program Director for Addictions Services at the Dunn Medical Center in Richmond, Indiana. She received her undergraduate degree in Social Work at St. Mary-of-the-Woods College in St. Mary-of-the-Woods, Indiana, and her MSW degree at Indiana University–Purdue in Indianapolis, Indiana. Shelly has served in a number of clinical and administrative positions over the last 20 years and as MSW Lecturer and Faculty at Indiana University at Indianapolis.

Shelley Schuurman, MSW, CSW, is a visiting Professor in the School of Social Work at Grand Valley State University in Grand Rapids, Michigan. She has practiced social work with families and children in a variety of settings, including residential treatment, foster care, prevention programs, and a psychiatric hospital. Her major areas of interest are vulnerable families as well as children and experiential learning in social work education. She currently teaches at the BSW and MSW levels at GVSU.

Kim Wetterman, MSW, graduated from the School of Social Work at Grand Valley State University in Grand Rapids, Michigan. She worked in domestic violence for one year and has experience working in the field of adoption as a resource to birth and adoptive families. She also provides workshops to medical personnel about identifying domestic violence in medical settings.

Heidi Weipert, MA, LLPC, NCC, provides counseling services in private practice at Morritt and Weipert Psychological Counseling Services, PLLC. Weipert works with crime victims, specifically women and children, and specializes in trauma recovery, abuse and neglect intervention, group work, and parenting. Weipert also has training in play and art therapy. She received her Master's Degree in Counseling from Central Michigan University and has over 12 years of professional experience. She is a board-eligible National Certified Counselor and certified by the Trauma and Loss Institute for Children.

Bibliography

Cournoyer, B. R. (2004). *The evidence-based social work skills book.* Boston: Allyn and Bacon.

Germain, C. B., & Gitterman, A. (1996). *The life model of social work practice* (2nd ed.). New York: Columbia University Press.

Gibbs, L. E. (2003). *Evidence-based practice for the helping professions: A practical guide with integrated multimedia.* Pacific Grove, CA: Brooks/Cole.

Harper, K. V., & Lantz, J. (1996). *Cross-cultural practice: Social work practice with diverse populations.* Chicago: Lyceum Books.

Johnson, J. L. (2004). *Fundamentals of substance abuse practice.* Pacific Grove, CA: Brooks/Cole.

Miller, W. R., & Rollnick, S. (2002). *Motivational interviewing: Preparing people to change addictive behavior* (2nd ed.). New York: Guilford Press.

Saleebey, D. (2002). *The strengths perspective in social work practice* (3rd ed.). Boston: Allyn and Bacon.

Timberlake, E. M., Farber, M. Z., & Sabatino, C. A. (2002). *The general method of social work practice: McMahon's generalist perspective* (4th ed.). Boston: Allyn and Bacon.

A Multi-Systemic Approach to Practice

Jerry L. Johnson & George Grant, Jr.

This is a practice-oriented text, designed to build practice skills with individuals, families, and groups. We intend to provide you the opportunity to study the process involved in treating real cases from the caseloads of experienced practitioners. Unlike other casebooks, we include fewer cases but provide substantially more detail in hopes of providing a realistic look into the thinking, planning, and approach of the practitioners/authors. We challenge you to study the authors' thinking and methods to understand their approach and then use critical thinking skills and the knowledge you have gained in your education and practice to propose alternative ways of treating the same clients. In other words, what would your course of action be if you were the primary practitioner responsible for these cases? Our hope is that this text provides a worthwhile and rigorous experience studying real cases as they progressed in practice.

Before proceeding to the cases, we include this chapter as an introduction to the Advanced Multi-Systemic (AMS) practice perspective. We decided to present this introduction with two primary goals in mind. First, we want you to use the information contained in this chapter to help assess and analyze the cases in this text. You will have the opportunity to complete a multi-systemic assessment, diagnoses, treatment, and intervention plan for each case. This chapter will provide the theoretical and practical basis for this exercise. Second, we hope you find that AMS makes conceptualizing cases clearer in your practice environment. We do not suggest that AMS is the only way, or even the best way, for every practitioner to conceptualize cases. We simply know, through experience, that AMS is an effective way to think about practice with client-systems of all sizes and configurations. While there are many approaches to practice, AMS offers an effective way to place clinical decisions in the context of client lives and experiences, making engagement and treatment productive for clients and practitioners.

Advanced Multi-Systemic (AMS) Practice

Sociological Roots

> Whether the point of interest is a great power state or a minor literary mood, a family, a prison, and a creed—these are the kinds of questions the best social analysts have asked. They are the intellectual pivots of classic studies of (person) in society—and they are the questions inevitably raised by any mind possessing the sociological imagination. For that imagination is the capacity to shift from one perspective to another—from the political to the psychological; from examination of a single family to comparative assessment of the national budgets of the world; from the theological school to the military establishment; from considerations of an oil industry to studies of contemporary poetry. It is the capacity to range from the most impersonal and remote transformations to the most intimate features of the human self—and see the relations between the two. Back of its use is always the urge to know the social and historical meaning of the individual in the society and in the period in which he (or she) has his quality and his (or her) being (Mills, 1959, p. 7; parentheses added).

Above, sociologist C. Wright Mills provided a seminal description of the sociological imagination. As it turns out, Mills's sociological imagination is also an apt description of AMS. Mills believed that linking people's "private troubles" to "public issues" (p. 2) was the most effective way to understand people and their issues, by placing them in historical context. It forces investigators to contextualize individuals and families in the framework of the larger social, political, economic, and historical environments in which they live. Ironically, this is also the goal of social work practice (Germain & Gitterman, 1996; Longres, 2000). Going further, Mills (1959) stated:

> We have come to know that every individual lives, from one generation to the next, in some society; he (or she) lives out a biography, and that he (or she) lives it out within some historical sequence. By the fact of his (or her) living he (or she) contributes, however minutely, to the shaping of this society and to the course of its history, even as he (or she) is made by society and by its historical push and shove (p. 6).

Again, Mills was not speaking as a social worker. He was an influential sociologist, speaking about a method of social research. In *The Sociological Imagination,* Mills (1959) proposed this as a method to understand the links between people, their daily lives, and their multi-systemic environment. Yet, while laying the theoretical groundwork for social research, Mills also provided the theoretical foundation for an effective approach to social work practice. We find four relevant points in *The Sociological Imagination* that translate directly to social work practice.

1. It is crucial to recognize the relationships between people's personal issues and strengths (private troubles) and the issues (political, economic, social, historical, and legal) and strengths of the multi-systemic environment (public issues) in which people live daily and across their lifespan. A multi-systemic understanding includes recognizing and integrating issues and strengths at the micro (individual, family, extended kin, etc.), mezzo (local community), and macro (state, regional, national, or international policy, legal, political, economic, and social) levels during client engagement, assessment, treatment, follow-up, and evaluation of practice.

2. This depth of understanding (by social workers and especially clients) can lead to change in people's lives. We speak here about second-order change, or significant change that makes a long-term difference in people's lives, change that helps people view themselves differently in relationship to their world. This level of change becomes possible when people make multi-systemic links in a way that makes sense to them (Freire, 1993). In other words, clients become "empowered" to change when they understand their life in the context of their world and realize that they have previously unforeseen or unimagined choices in how they live, think, believe, and act.

3. Any assessment and/or clinical diagnoses that exclude multi-systemic links do not provide a holistic picture of people's lives, their troubles and/or strengths. In sociology, this leads to a reductionist view of people and society, while in social work it reduces the likelihood that services will be provided (or received by clients) in a way that addresses client problems and utilizes client strengths in a meaningful way. The opportunity for change is reduced whenever client life history is overlooked because it does not fit, or is not called for, in a practitioner's preferred method of helping or because of shortcuts many people believe are needed in a managed care environment. Practitioners cannot learn too much about their clients, their lives, and their attitudes, beliefs, and values as they relate to the private troubles presented in treatment.

4. Inherent in AMS and foundational to achieving all that was discussed above is practitioners' ability to rapidly develop rapport with clients that leads to engagement in treatment. In this text, client engagement

> occurs when you develop, in collaboration with clients, a trusting and open professional relationship that promotes hope and presents viable prospects for change. Successful engagement occurs when you create a social context in which vulnerable people (who often hold jaded attitudes toward helping professionals) can share their innermost feelings, as well as their most embarrassing and shameful behavior, with you, a *total stranger* (Johnson, 2004, p. 93; emphasis in original).

AMS Overview

First, we should define two important terms that comprise AMS. Understanding these terms is important because they provide the foundation for understanding the language and concepts used throughout the remainder of this chapter.

1. Advanced. According to Derezotes (2000), "the most advanced theory is also the most inclusive" (p. viii). AMS is advanced because it is inclusive. It requires responsible practitioners, in positions of responsibility (perhaps as solo practitioners), to acquire a depth of knowledge, skills, and self-awareness that allows for an inclusive application of knowledge acquired in the areas of human behavior in the social environment, social welfare policy, social research and practice evaluation, and multiple practice methods and approaches in service of clients and client systems of various sizes, types, and configurations.

AMS practitioners are expected to have the most inclusive preparation possible, "both the broad generalist base of knowledge, skills, and values and an in-depth proficiency in practice . . . with selected social work methods and populations" (Derezotes, 2000, p. xii). Hence, advanced practitioners are well trained, have in-depth knowledge, and are often in positions of being responsible for clients as primary practitioners. They are afforded the responsibility for engaging, assessing, intervening, and evaluating practice, ensuring that their clients are ethically treated in a way that is culturally competent and respectful of their clients' worldview. In other words, AMS practitioners develop the knowledge, skills, and values needed to be leaders in their organizations, communities, the social work profession, and especially the treatment of their clients. The remainder of this chapter explains why AMS is an advanced approach to practice.

2. Multi-Systemic. From the earliest moments in their education, social workers learn a systems perspective that emphasizes the connectedness between people and their problems to the complex interrelationships that exist in their clients' world (Timberlake, Farber, & Sabatino, 2002). To explain these connections, systems theory emphasizes three important concepts: wholeness, relationships, and homeostasis. Wholeness refers to the notion that the various parts or elements (subsystems) of a system interact to form a whole that best describes the system in question. This concept asserts that no system can be understood or explained unless the connectedness of the subsystems to the whole are understood or explained. In other words, the whole is greater than the sum of its parts. Moreover, systems theory also posits that change in one subsystem will affect change in the system as a whole.

In terms of systems theory, relationship refers to the patterns of interaction and overall structures that exist within and between subsystems. The nature of these relationships is more important than the system itself. That is, when trying to understand or explain a system (individual, family, or organization), how subsystems connect through relationships, the characteristics of the relationships between subsystems, and how the subsystems interact provide clues to understanding the system as a whole. Hence, the application of systems theory is primarily based on understanding relationships. As someone once said about systems theory, in systems problems occur between people and subsystems (relationships), not "in" them. People's internal problems relate to the nature of the relationships in the systems where they live and interact.

Homeostasis refers to the notion that most living systems work to maintain and preserve the existing system, or the status quo. For example, family members often assume roles that serve to protect and maintain family stability, often at the expense of "needed" change. The same can be said for organizations or groups. The natural tendency toward homeostasis in systems represents what we call the "dilemma of change" (Johnson, 2004). This can best be described as the apparent conflict, or what appears to be client resistance or lack of motivation, that often occurs when clients approach moments of significant change. Systems of all types and configurations struggle with the dilemma of change: should they change to the unknown or remain the same, even if the status quo is unhealthy or unproductive? Put differently, systems strive for stability, even at the expense of health and well-being of individual members and/or the system itself.

What do we mean, then, by the term *multi-systemic*? Clients (individuals, families, etc.) are systems that interact with a number of different systems simultaneously. These systems exist and interact at multiple levels, ranging from the micro level (individual and families) to the mezzo level (local community, institutions, organizations, the practitioner and their agency, etc.) to the macro level (culture, laws and policy, politics, oppression and discrimination, international events, etc.). The ways these various systems come together, interact, and adapt, along with the relationships that exist within and between each system, work together to comprise the "whole" that is the client, or client-system. In practice, the client (individual, couple, family, etc.) is not the "system," but one of many interacting subsystems in a maze of other subsystems constantly interacting to create the system—the client plus elements from multiple subsystems at each level. It would be a mistake to view the client as the whole system. Clients are but one facet of a multidimensional and multi-level system comprised of the client and various other subsystems at the micro, mezzo, and macro levels.

Therefore, the term *multi-systemic* refers to the nature of a system comprised of the various multi-level subsystems described above. A multi-systemic perspective recognizes that clients are *one part or subsystem* in relationship with other subsystemic influences occurring on different levels. This level of understanding—the system as the whole produced through multi-systemic subsystem interactions—is the main unit of investigation for practice. As stated above, it is narrow to consider the client as a functioning independent system with peripheral involvement with other systems existing outside of an intimate world. These issues and relationships work together to help shape and mold the client, who in turn shapes and molds relationships to the other subsystems. Yet, the person of the client is but one part of the system in question during practice.

AMS provides an organized framework for gathering, conceptualizing, and analyzing multi-systemic client data and for proceeding with the helping process. It defines the difference between social work and other disciplines in the helping professions at the level of theory and practice. How, you ask? Unlike other professional disciplines that tend to focus on one or a few domains (e.g., psychology, medicine), AMS provides a comprehensive and holistic "picture" of clients or client-systems in the context of their environment by considering information about multiple personal and systemic domains simultaneously.

Resting on the generalist foundation taught in all accredited Council on Social Work Education (CSWE) undergraduate and foundation-level graduate programs, AMS requires practitioners to contextualize client issues in the context of the multiple interactions that occur between the client/client-system and the social, economic, legal, political, and physical environments in which the client lives. It is a unifying perspective based on the client's life, history, and culture that guides the process of collecting and analyzing client life information and intervening to promote personal choice through a comprehensive multi-systemic framework. Beginning with culturally competent client engagement, a comprehensive multi-systemic assessment points toward a holistically based treatment plan that requires practitioners to select and utilize appropriate practice theories, models, and methods—or combinations thereof—that best fit the client's unique circumstances and needs.

AMS is not a practice theory, model, or method itself. It is a perspective or framework for conceptualizing client-systems. It relies on the practitioner's ability to use a variety of theories, models, and methods and to incorporate knowledge from human behavior, social policy, research/evaluation, and practice into their routine approach with clients. For example, an AMS practitioner will have the skills to apply different approaches to individual treatment (client-centered, cognitive-behavioral, etc.) and family treatment (structural, narrative, Bowenian, etc.); work with couples and in groups; arrange for specialized care if needed; and work as an advocate on behalf of their client. It may also require practitioners to treat clients in a multi-modal approach (i.e., individual and group treatments simultaneously).

Practitioners must know not only how to apply different approaches but also how to determine, primarily through the early engagement and assessment process, which theory, model, or approach (direct or indirect, for example) would work best for a particular client. Hence, successful practice using AMS relies heavily on the practitioner's ability to competently engage and multi-systemically assess client problems and strengths. Practitioners must simultaneously develop a sense of their clients' personal interaction and relationship style—especially related to how they relate to authority figures—when determining which approach would best suit the clients. For example, a reserved, quiet, or thoughtful client or someone who lacks assertiveness may not be well served by a directive, confrontational approach, regardless of the practitioner's preference. Moreover, AMS practitioners rely on professional practice research and outcome studies to help determine which approach or intervention package might work best for particular clients and/or client-systems. AMS expects practitioners to know how to find and evaluate practice research in their practice areas or specialties.

Elements of the Advanced Multi-Systemic Approach to Social Work Practice

The advanced multi-systemic approach entails the following seven distinct yet integrated elements of theory and practice. Each is explained below.

Ecological Systems Perspective

One important subcategory of systems therapy for social work is the ecological systems perspective. This perspective combines important concepts from the science of ecology and general systems theory in a way of viewing client problems and strengths in social work practice. In recent years, it has become the prevailing perspective for social work practice (Miley, O'Melia, & DuBois, 2004). The ecological systems perspective—sometimes referred to as the ecosystems perspective—is a useful metaphor for guiding social workers as they think about cases (Germain & Gitterman, 1980).

Ecology focuses on how subsystems work together and adapt. In ecology, adaptation is "a dynamic process between people and their environments as people grow, achieve competence, and make contributions to others" (Greif, 1986, p. 225). Insight from ecology leads to an analysis of how people fit within their environment and what adaptations are made in the fit between people and their environments. Problems develop as a function of inadequate or improper adaptation or fit between people and their environments.

General systems theory focuses on how human systems interact. It focuses specifically on how people grow, survive, change, and achieve stability or instability in the complex world of multiple systemic interactions (Miley, O'Melia, & DuBois, 2004). General systems theory has contributed significantly to the growth of the family therapy field and to how social workers understand their clients.

Together, ecology and general systems theory evolved into what social workers know as the ecological systems perspective. The ecological systems perspective provides a systemic framework for understanding the many ways that persons and environments interact. Accordingly, individuals and their individual circumstances can be understood in the context of these interactions. The ecological systems perspective provides an important part of the foundation for AMS. Miley, O'Melia, and DuBois (2004, p. 33) provide an excellent summary of the ecological systems perspective. They suggest that it

1. Presents a dynamic view of human beings as systems interaction in context.
2. Emphasizes the significance of human system interactions.
3. Traces how human behavior and interaction develop over time in response to internal and external forces.
4. Describes current behavior as an adaptive fit of "persons in situations."
5. Conceptualizes all interaction as adaptive or logical in context.

6. Reveals multiple options for change within persons, their social groups, and in their social and physical environments.

Social Constructionism

To maintain AMS as an inclusive practice approach, we need to build on the ecological systems perspective by including ideas derived from social constructionism. Social constructionism builds on the ecological systems perspective by introducing ideas about how people define themselves and their environment. Social constructionism also, by definition, introduces the role of culture in the meaning people give to themselves and other systems in their multi-systemic environments. The ecological systems perspective discusses relationships at the systemic level. Social constructionism introduces meaning and value into the equation, allowing for a deeper understanding and appreciation of the nature of multi-systemic relationships and adaptations.

Usually, people assume that reality is something "out there" that hits them in the face, something that independently exists, and people must learn to "deal with it." Social constructionism posits something different. Evolving as a critique of the "one reality" belief system, social constructionism points out that the world is comprised of multiple realities. People define their own reality and then live within that definition. Accordingly, the definition of reality will be different for everyone. Hence, social constructionism deals primarily with meaning, or the systemic processes by which people come to define themselves in their social world. As sociologist W. I. Thomas said, in what has become known as the Thomas Theorem, "If people define situations as real, they are real in their consequences."

For example, some people believe that they can influence the way computerized slot machines pay out winnings by the way they sit, the feeling they get from the machine as they look at it in the casino, by the clothes they are wearing, or by how they trigger the machine, either by pushing the button or pulling the handle. Likewise, many athletes believe that a particular article of clothing, a routine for getting dressed, and/or a certain pregame meal dictates the quality of their athletic prowess that day.

Illogical to most people, the belief that they can influence a computerized machine, that the machine emits feelings, or that an article of clothing dictates athletic prowess is real to some people. For these people, their beliefs influence the way they live. Perhaps you have ideas or "superstitions" that you believe influence how your life goes on a particular day. This is a common occurrence. You are not necessarily out of touch with objective reality. While people may know, at some level, that slot machines pay according to preset computerized odds or that athletic prowess has nothing to do with dressing routines, the belief systems continue. What dictates the behavior and beliefs discussed above or in daily "superstitions" have nothing to do with objective reality and everything to do with people's subjective reality.

Subjective reality—or a person's learned definition of the situation—overrides objectivity and helps determine how people behave and/or what they believe.

While these examples may be simplistic, according to social constructionism, the same processes influence everyone—always. In practice, understanding that people's behavior does not depend on the objective existence of something, but on their subjective interpretation of it, is crucial to effective application of AMS. This knowledge is most helpful during client engagement. If practitioners remember that practice is about understanding people's perceptions and not objective reality, they reduce the likelihood that clients will feel misunderstood, there will be fewer disagreements, and it will be easier to avoid the trap of defining normal behavior as client resistance or a diagnosable mental disorder. This perspective contributes to a professional relationship based in the client's life and belief systems, consistent with their worldview, and culturally appropriate for the client. Being mindful that the definitions people learn from their culture underlies not only what they do but also what they perceive, feel, and think places practitioners on the correct path to "start where the client is." Social constructionism emphasizes the cultural uniqueness of each client and/or client-system and the need to understand each client and/or client-system in their own context and belief systems, not the practitioner's context or belief systems.

Social constructionism also posits that different people attribute different meaning to the same events, because the interactional contexts and the way individuals interpret these contexts are different for everyone, even within the same family or community. One cannot assume that people raised in the same family will define their social world similarly. Individuals, in the context of their environments, derive meaning through a complex process of individual interpretation. This is how siblings from the same family can be so different, almost as if they did not grow up in the same family. For example, the sound of gunfire in the middle of the night may be frightening or normal, depending upon where a person resides and what is routine and accepted in their specific environment. Moreover, simply because some members of a family or community understand nightly gunfire as normal does not mean that others in the same family or community will feel the same.

Additionally, social constructionism examines how people construct meaning with language and established or evolving cultural beliefs. For example, alcohol consumption is defined as problematic depending upon how the concept of "alcohol problem" is socially constructed in specific environments. Clients from so-called drinking cultures may define drinking six alcoholic drinks daily as normal, while someone from a different cultural background may see this level of consumption as problematic. One of the authors worked in Russia and found an issue that demonstrates this point explicitly. Colleagues in Russia stated rather emphatically that consuming one "bottle" (approximately a U.S. pint) of vodka per day was acceptable and normal. People that consume more than one bottle per day were defined as having a drinking problem. The same level of consumption in the United States would be considered by most as clear evidence of problem drinking.

Biopsychosocial Perspective

Alone, the ecological systems perspective, even with the addition of social constructionism, does not provide the basis for the holistic understanding required by AMS. While it provides a multi-systemic lens, the ecological systems perspective focuses mostly on externals, that is, how people interact and adapt to their environments and how environments interact and adapt to people. Yet, much of what practitioners consider "clinical" focuses on "internals" or human psychological and emotional functioning. Therefore, the ecological systems perspective provides only one part of the holistic picture required by the advanced multi-systemic approach. By adding the biopsychosocial perspective, practitioners can consider the internal workings of human beings to help explain how external and internal subsystems interact.

What is the biopsychosocial perspective? It is a theoretical perspective that considers how human biological, psychological, and social-functioning subsystems interact to account for how people live in their environment. Similar to social systems, human beings are also multidimensional systems comprised of multiple subsystems constantly interacting in its environment, the human body. The biopsychosocial perspective applies multi-systemic thinking to individual human beings.

Several elements comprise the biopsychosocial perspective. Longres (2000) identifies two dimensions of individual functioning, the biophysical and the psychological, subdividing the psychological into three sub-dimensions: the cognitive, affective, and behavioral. Elsewhere, we added the spiritual/existential dimension to this conception (Johnson, 2004). Understanding how the biological, psychological, spiritual and existential, and social subsystems interact is instrumental in developing an appreciation of how individuals influence and are influenced by their social systemic environments. Realizing that each of these dimensions interacts with external social and environmental systems allows practitioners to enlarge their frame of reference, leading to a more holistic multi-systemic view of clients and client-systems.

Strengths/Empowerment Perspective

Over the last few years, the strengths perspective has emerged as an important part of social work theory and practice. The strengths perspective represents a significant change in how social workers conceptualize clients and client-systems. According to Saleebey (2002), it is "a versatile practice approach, relying heavily on ingenuity and creativity. . . . Rather than focusing on problems, your eye turns toward possibility" (p. 1). Strengths-based practitioners believe in the power of possibility and hope in helping people overcome problems by focusing on, locating, and supporting existing personal or systemic strengths and resiliencies. The strengths perspective is based on the belief that people, regardless of the severity of their problems, have the capabilities and resources to play an active role in helping solve their own problems. The practitioner's role is to engage clients in a way that unleashes these capabilities and resources toward solving problems and changing lives.

Empowerment

Any discussion of strengths-based approaches must also consider empowerment as an instrumental element of the approach. Empowerment, as a term in social work, has evolved over the years. We choose a definition of empowerment that focuses on power: internal, interpersonal, and environmental (Parsons, Gutierrez, & Cox, 1998). According to Parsons, Gutierrez, and Cox (1998),

> In its most positive sense, power is (1) the ability to influence the course of one's life, (2) an expression of self worth, (3) the capacity to work with others to control aspects of public life, and (4) access to the mechanisms of public decision making. When used negatively, though, it can also block opportunities for stigmatized groups, exclude others and their concerns from decision making, and be a way to control others (p. 8).

Hence, empowerment in practice is a process (Parsons, Gutierrez, and Cox, 1998) firmly grounded in ecological systems and strength-based approaches that focus on gaining power by individuals, families, groups, organizations, or communities. It is based on two related assumptions: (1) all human beings are potentially competent, even in extremely challenging situations, and (2) all human beings are subject to various degrees of powerlessness (Cox & Parsons, 1994, p. 17) and oppression (Freire, 1993). People internalize their sense of powerlessness and oppression in a way that their definition of self in the world is limited, often eliminating any notion that they can act in their own behalf in a positive manner.

An empowerment approach makes practical connections between power and powerlessness. It illuminates how these factors interact to influence clients in their daily life. Empowerment is not achieved through a single intervention, nor is it something that can be "done" to another. Empowerment does not occur through neglect or by simply giving responsibility for their life and well-being to the poor or troubled, allowing them to be "free" from government regulation, support, or professional assistance. In other words, empowerment of disenfranchised groups does not occur simply by dismantling systems (such as the welfare system) to allow these groups or individuals to take responsibility for themselves. Hence, empowerment does not preclude helping.

Consistent with our definition, empowerment develops through the approach taken toward helping, not the act of helping itself. Empowerment is a sense of gained or regained power that someone attains in their life that provides the foundation for change in the short term and that stimulates belief in their ability to positively influence their lives over the long term. Empowerment occurs as a function of the long-term approach of the practitioner and the professional relationship developed between practitioner and client. One cannot provide an empowering context through a constant focus on problems, deficits, inadequacies, negative labeling, and dependency.

The Power of Choice

Choice is an instrumental part of strengths-based and empowerment approaches, by recognizing that people, because of inherent strengths and capabilities, can make informed choices about their lives, just like people who are not clients. Practitioners work toward offering people choices about how they define their lives and problems, the extent to which they want to address their problems, and the means or mechanisms through which change should occur. Clients become active and instrumental partners in the helping process. They are not passive vessels, waiting for practitioners to "change them" through some crafty intervention or technique.

We are not talking about the false choices sometimes given to clients by practitioners. For example, clients with substance abuse problems are often told that they must either abstain or leave treatment. Most practitioners ignore, or use as evidence of denial, client requests to attempt so-called controlled use. If practitioners were interested in offering true choice, they would work with these clients toward their controlled-drinking goal in an effort to reduce the potential harm that may result from their use of substances (Johnson, 2004; van Wormer & Davis, 2003), even if the practitioner believes that controlled drinking is not possible. Abstinence would become the goal only when their clients choose to include it as a goal.

Client Engagement as Cultural Competence

Empowerment (choice) occurs through a process of culturally competent client engagement, created by identifying strengths, generating dialogue targeted at revealing the extent of people's oppression (Freire, 1993), and respecting their right to make informed choices in their lives. Accordingly, empowerment is the "transformation from individual and collective powerlessness to personal, political, and cultural power" (GlenMaye, 1998, p. 29), through a strengths-based relationship with a professional helper.

Successful application of AMS requires the ability to engage clients in open and trusting professional relationships. The skills needed to engage clients from different backgrounds and with different personal and cultural histories are what drives practice, what determines the difference between successful and unsuccessful practice. Advanced client engagement skills allow the practitioner to elicit in-depth multi-systemic information in a dialogue between client and practitioner (Johnson, 2004), providing the foundation for strengths-based client empowerment leading to change.

Earlier, we defined client engagement as a mutual process occurring between clients and practitioners in a professional context, created by practitioners. In other words, creating the professional space and open atmosphere that allow engagement to flourish is the primary responsibility of the practitioner, not the client. Practitioners must have the skills and knowledge to adjust their approach toward specific clients and the clients' cultural context and not *vice versa*. Clients do not adjust to us and our beliefs, values, and practices—we adjust to them. When that occurs, the foundation exists for client engagement. By definition, relationships of this nature must be performed in a culturally competent manner. Yet, what does this mean?

Over the last two decades, social work and other helping professions have been concerned with cultural competence in practice (Fong, 2001). Beginning in the late 1970s the professional literature has been replete with ideas, definitions, and practice models designed to increase cultural awareness and promote culturally appropriate practice methods. Yet, despite the attention given to the issue, there remains confusion about how to define and teach culturally competent practice.

Structural and Historical Systems of Oppression: Who Holds the Power?

Often embedded in laws, policies, and social institutions are oppressive influences such as racism, sexism, homophobia, and classism, to name a few. These structural issues play a significant role in the lives of clients (through maltreatment and discrimination) and in social work practice. How people are treated (or how they internalize historical treatment of self, family, friends, and/or ancestors) shapes how they believe, think, and act in the present. Oppression affects how they perceive what others feel about them, how they view the world and their place in it, and how receptive they are to professional service providers. Therefore, culturally competent practice must consider the impact of structural systems of oppression and injustice on clients, their problems, strengths, and potential for change.

Oppression is a by-product of socially constructed notions of power, privilege, control, and hierarchies of difference. As stated above, it is created and maintained by differences in power. By definition, those who have power can force people to abide by the rules, standards, and actions the powerful deem worthwhile, mandatory, or acceptable. Those who hold power can enforce particular worldviews; deny equal access and opportunity to housing, employment, or health care; define right and wrong, normal and abnormal; and imprison, confine, and/or commit physical, emotional, or mental violence against the powerless (McLaren, 1995; Freire, 1993). Most importantly, power permits the holder to "set the very terms of power" (Appleby, 2001, p. 37). It defines the interaction between the oppressed and the oppressor, and between the social worker and client.

Social institutions and practices are developed and maintained by the dominant culture to meet *its* needs and maintain *its* power. Everything and everybody are judged and classified accordingly. Even when the majority culture develops programs or engages in helping activities, these efforts will not include measures that threaten the dominant group's position at the top of the social hierarchy (Freire, 1993). For example, Kozol (1991) wrote eloquently about how public schools fail by design, while Freire (1993) wrote about how state welfare and private charity provide short-term assistance while ensuring that there are not enough resources to lift people permanently out of poverty.

Oppression is neither an academic nor a theoretical consideration; it is not a faded relic of a bygone era. Racism did not end with the civil rights movement, and sexism was not eradicated by the feminist movement. Understanding how systems of oppression work in people's lives is of paramount importance for every individual and family seeking professional help, including those who belong to the *same* race, gender, and class as the practitioner. No two individuals, regardless of their personal demographics, experience the world in the same way. Often, clients are treated ineffectively by professional helpers who mistakenly believe that people who look or act the same will experience the world in similar ways. These workers base their assumptions about clients on stereotypic descriptions of culture, lifestyle, beliefs and practices. They take group-level data (e.g., many African American adolescents join gangs because of broken families and poverty) and assume that *all* African American teenagers are gang members from single-parent families. Social work values and ethics demand a higher standard, one that compels us to go beyond stereotypes. Our job is to discover, understand, and utilize personal differences in the assessment and treatment process to benefit clients, not use differences as a way of limiting clients' potential for health and well-being.

We cannot accurately assess or treat people without considering the effects of oppression related to race, ethnicity, culture, sexual preference, gender, or physical/emotional status. We need to understand how oppression influences our clients' beliefs about problems and potential approaches to problem solving and how it determines what kind of support they can expect to receive if they decide to seek help. For example, despite the widely held belief that chemical dependency is an equal opportunity disease (Gordon, 1993), it is clear that some people are more vulnerable than others. While some of the general themes of chemical dependency may appear universal, each client is unique. That is, an individual's dependency results from personal behavior, culture (including the history of one's culture), past experiences, and family interacting with larger social systems that provide opportunities or impose limits on the individual (Johnson, 2000).

Systems of oppression ensure unequal access to resources for certain individuals, families, and communities. However, while all oppressed people are similar in that they lack the power to define their place in the social hierarchy, oppression based on race, gender, sexual orientation, class, and other social factors is expressed in a variety of ways. Learning about cultural nuances is important in client assessment, treatment planning, and treatment (Lum, 1999). According to Pinderhughes (1989), there is no such thing as culture-free service delivery. Cultural differences between clients and social workers in terms of values, norms, beliefs, attitudes, lifestyles, and life opportunities affect every aspect of practice.

What Is Culture?

Many different concepts of culture are used in social work, sociology, and anthropology. Smelser (1992) considers culture a "system of patterned values, meanings, and beliefs that give cognitive structure to the world, provide a basis for coordinating and controlling human interactions, and constitute a link as the system is transmitted from one generation to another" (p. 11). Geertz (1973) regarded culture as simultaneously a product of and a guide to people searching for organized categories and interpretations that provide a meaningful experiential link to their social life. Building upon these two ideas, in this book we abide by the following definition of culture proposed elsewhere (Johnson, 2000):

> Culture is historical, bound up in traditions and practices passed through generations; memories of events—real or imagined—that define a people and their worldview. (Culture) is viewed as collective subjectivity, or a way of life adopted by a community that ultimately defines their worldview (p. 121).

Consistent with this definition, the collective subjectivities called culture are pervasive forces in the way people interact, believe, think, feel, and act in their social world. Culture plays a significant role in shaping how people view the world. As a historical force, in part built on ideas, definitions, and events passed through generations, culture also defines people's level of social acceptance by the wider community; shapes how people live, think, and act; and influences how people perceive that others feel about them and how they view the world and their place in it. Thus, it is impossible to understand a client without grasping their cultural foundations.

Cultural Competence

As stated earlier, over the years many different ideas and definitions of what constitutes culturally competent practice have developed, as indicated by the growth of the professional literature since the late 1970s. To date, focus has primarily been placed in two areas: (1) the need for practitioners to be aware of their own cultural beliefs, ideas, and identities leading to cultural sensitivity, and (2) learning factual and descriptive information about various ethnic and racial groups based mostly on group-level survey data and analyses. Fong (2001) suggests that culture is often considered "tangential" to individual functioning and not central to the client's functioning (p. 5).

To address this issue, Fong (2001) builds on Lum's (1999) culturally competent practice model that focuses on four areas: (1) cultural awareness, (2) knowledge acquisition, (3) skill development, and (4) inductive learning. Besides inductive learning, Lum's model places focus mainly on practitioners in perpetual self-awareness, gaining knowledge about cultures, and skill building. While these are important ideas for cultural competence, Fong (2001) calls for a shift in thinking and practice, "to provide a culturally competent service focused solely on the client rather than the social worker and what he or she brings to the awareness of ethnicity" (p. 5). Fong (2001) suggests an "extension" (p. 6) of Lum's model by turning the focus of each of the four elements away from the practitioner toward the client. For example, cultural awareness changes from a practitioner focus to "the social worker's understanding and the identification of the critical cultural values important to the client system and to themselves" (p. 6). This change allows Fong (2001) to remain consistent with the stated definition of culturally competent practice, insisting that practitioners,

> operating from an empowerment, strengths, and ecological framework, provide services, conduct assessments, and implement interventions that are reflective of the clients' cultural values and norms, congruent with their natural help-seeking behaviors, and inclusive of existing indigenous solutions (p. 1).

While we agree with the idea that "to be culturally competent is to know the cultural values of the client system and to use them in planning and implementing services" (Fong, 2001, p. 6), we want to make this shift the main point of a culturally competent model of client engagement. That is, beyond what should or must occur, we believe that professional education and training must focus on the skills of culturally competent client engagement that are necessary to make this happen, a model that places individual client cultural information at the center of practice. We agree with Fong (2001) that having culturally sensitive or culturally aware practitioners is not nearly enough. Practitioner self-awareness and knowledge of different cultures do not constitute cultural competence. We strive to find a method for reaching this worthy goal.

The central issue revolves around practitioners participating in inductive learning and the skills of grounded theory. In other words, regardless of practitioner beliefs, awarenesses, or sensitivities, their job is to learn about and understand their client's world and to "ground" their theory of practice in the cultural context of their client. They develop a unique theory of human behavior in a multi-systemic context for every client. Culturally competent client engagement does not happen by assessing the extent to which client lives "fit" within existing theory and knowledge about reality, most of which is middle-class and Eurocentric at its core. Cultural competence (Johnson, 2004)

> *begins* with learning about different cultures, races, personal circumstances, and structural mechanisms of oppression. It *occurs* when practitioners master the interpersonal skills needed to move beyond general descriptions of a specific culture or race to learn specific individual, family, group, or community interpretations of culture, ethnicity, and race. The culturally competent practitioner knows that within each culture are individually interpreted and practiced thoughts, beliefs, and behaviors that may or may not be consistent with group-level information. That is, there is tremendous diversity within groups, as well as between them. Individuals are unique unto themselves, not simply interchangeable members of a specific culture, ethnicity, or race who naturally abide by the group-level norms often taught on graduate and undergraduate courses on human diversity (p. 105).

Culturally competent client engagement revolves around the practitioner's ability to create a relationship, through the professional use of self, based in true dialogue (Freire, 1993; Johnson, 2004). We define dialogue as "a joint endeavor, developed between people (in this case, practitioner and client) that move clients from their current state of hopelessness to a more hopeful, motivated position in their world" (Johnson, 2004, p. 97). Elsewhere (Johnson, 2004), we detailed a model of culturally competent engagement based on Freire's (1993) definitions of oppression, communication, dialogue, practitioner self-work, and the ability to exhibit worldview respect, hope, humility, trust, and empathy.

To investigate culture in a competent manner is to take a comprehensive look into people's worldview—to discover what they believe about the world and their place in it. It goes beyond race and ethnicity (although these are important issues) into how culture determines thoughts, feelings, and behaviors in daily life. This includes what culture says about people's problems; culturally appropriate strengths and resources; the impact of gender on these issues; and what it means to seek professional help (Leigh, 1998).

The larger questions to be answered are how clients uniquely and individually interpret their culture; how their beliefs, attitudes, and behaviors are shaped by that interpretation; and how these cultural beliefs and practices affect daily life and determine lifestyle in the context of the larger community. Additionally, based on their cultural membership, beliefs, and practices, practitioners need to discover the potential and real barriers faced by clients in the world. For many clients, they are part of non-majority cultures whose issues generated by social systems of oppression such as racism, sexism, homophobia, and ethnocentrism expose them to limitations and barriers that others do not face.

What is the value of culturally competent client engagement? Helping clients discuss their attitudes, beliefs, and behaviors in the context of their culture—including their religious or spiritual belief systems—offers valuable information about their worldview, sense of social and spiritual connection, and/or practical involvement in their social world. Moreover, establishing connections between their unique interpretation of their culture and their daily life provides vital clues about people's belief systems, attitudes, expectations (social construction of reality), and explanation of behaviors that cannot be understood outside the context of their socially constructed interpretation of culture.

A Cautionary Note

It is easy to remember to ask about culture when clients are obviously different (e.g., different races, countries of origin). However, many practitioners forgo cultural investigation with clients they consider to have the same cultural background as themselves. For example, the search for differences between European-Americans with Christian beliefs—if the social worker shares these characteristics—gets lost in mutual assumptions, based on the misguided belief that there are no important differences between them. The same is often true when clients and practitioners come from the same racial, cultural, or lifestyle backgrounds (e.g., African American practitioner and client, gay practitioner and gay client). Culturally competent practice means that practitioners are always interested in people's individual interpretation of their culture and their subjective definitions of reality, whether potential differences are readily apparent or not. Practitioners must be diligent to explore culture with clients who appear to be from the same background as themselves, just as they would with people who are obviously from different cultural, racial, ethnic, or religious backgrounds.

Multiple Theories and Methods

No single theory, model, or method is best suited to meet the needs of all clients (Miley, O'Melia, & DuBois, 2004). Consistent with this statement, one of the hallmarks of AMS is the expectation that practitioners must determine which theory, model, or method will best suit a particular client. Choosing from a range of approaches and interventions, AMS practitioners develop the skills and abilities, based on the client's life, history, culture, and style, to (1) determine which treatment approach (theory and/or method) would best suit their needs and achieve the desired outcome, (2) determine which modality or modalities (individual, family, group treatment, etc.) will best meet the need of their clients, and (3) conduct treatment according to their informed clinical decisions.

Over the last 20 years or so, graduate social work education has tended toward practice specialization through concentration-based curricula. Many graduate schools of social work build on the generalist foundation by insisting that students focus on learning specific practice models or theories (disease, cognitive-behavioral, psychoanalysis, etc.) and/or specific practice methods (individual, family, group, etc.), often at the exclusion of other methods or models. For example, students often enter the field intent on doing therapy with individuals, say, from a cognitive-behavioral approach only.

This trend encourages practitioners to believe that one approach or theory best represents the "Truth." Truth, in this sense, is the belief that one theory or approach works best for most people, most of the time. It helps create a practice scenario that leads practitioners to use their chosen approach with every client they treat. Therefore, practice becomes a process of the practitioner forcing clients to adjust to the practitioner's beliefs and expectations about the nature of problems, the course of treatment, and definition of positive versus negative outcomes. From this perspective, what is best for clients is determined by what the practitioner believes is best, not on what clients believe is in their best interest.

Some practitioners take their belief in the Truth of a particular theory or method to extremes. They believe that one model or theory works best for all people, all the time. We found this to be common in the family therapy field, whereby some true believers insist that everyone needs family therapy—so that is all they offer. What's worse is that many of these same practitioners know and use only one particular family therapy theory and model. The "true believer" approach can cause problems, especially for clients. For example, when clients do not respond to treatment, instead of looking to other approaches, true believers simply prescribe more of the method that did not work in the first place. If a more intensive application of the method does not work, then the client's "lack of readiness" for treatment, resistance, or denial becomes the culprit. These practitioners usually give little thought to their practice approach or personal style and its impact on client "readiness" for treatment. They fail to examine the role their personal style, beliefs, attitudes, and practices have in creating the context that led to clients not succeeding in treatment.

Each practice theory and model has a relatively unique way of defining client problems, practitioner method and approach, interventions, and what constitutes successful outcome. For practitioners to believe that one theory or model is true, even if only for most people, they must believe in the universality of problems, methods and approaches, interventions, and successful outcome criteria. This contradicts the definition of theory. While being far from a concrete representation of the truth, a theory is a set of myths, expectations, guesses, and conjectures about what might be true (Best & Kellner, 1991). A theory is hypothetical, a set of ideas and explanations that need proving. No single theory can explain everything. According to Popper (1994), a theory "always remains guesswork, and there is no theory that is not beset with problems" (p. 157). As such, treatment specialization can—although not always—encourage people to believe they have found the Truth where little truth exists.

Practitioners using an AMS perspective come to believe that some element of every established practice model, method, or theory may be helpful. Accordingly, every model, method, or theory can be adapted and used in a multi-systemic practice framework. As an AMS practitioner, one neither accepts any single model fully nor disregards a model entirely if there is potential for helping a client succeed in a way that is compatible with professional social work values and ethics. These practitioners hone their critical thinking skills (Gambrill, 1997, 1990) and apply them in practice, particularly as it pertains to treatment theories, models, and methods. In the context of evidence-based practice (Cournoyer, 2004; Gibbs, 2003), sharpened critical thinking skills allow practitioners to closely read and evaluate practice theories, research, or case reports to recognize the strengths, weaknesses, and contradictions in theories, models, and/or policy related to social work practice.

Informed Eclecticism

The goal of AMS is for practitioners to develop an approach we call *informed eclecticism.* Informed eclecticism allows the use of multiple methods, interventions, and approaches in the context of practice (1) that is held together by a perspective or approach that provides consistency; (2) that makes practice choices in a way that makes sense in a particular client's life; and (3) that is based, whenever possible, on the latest evidence about its efficacy with particular problems and particular clients. While it is often best to rely on empirical evidence, this data is in its infancy. AMS does not preclude the use of informed practice wisdom and personal creativity in developing intervention plans and approaches. It is up to practitioners to ensure that any treatment based in practice wisdom or that is creatively generated be discussed with colleagues, supervisors, or consultants to ensure theoretical consistency and that it fits within the code of professional ethics.

Informed eclecticism is different from the routine definition of eclecticism—the use of whatever theory, model, or method works best for their clients. While this is the goal of AMS practice specifically and social work practice in general (Timberlake, Farber, & Sabatino, 2002), it is an elusive goal indeed. Informed eclecticism often gets lost in a practitioner's quest to find something that "works." According to Gambrill (1997), eclecticism is "the view that we should adopt whatever theories or methodologies are useful in inquiry, no matter what their source and without worry about their consistency" (p. 93). The most important word in Gambrill's statement is "consistency." While there are practitioners who have managed to develop a consistent, organized, and holistic version of informed eclecticism, this is not the norm.

Too often, uninformed eclecticism resembles the following. A practitioner specializes by modality (individual therapy) and uses a variety of modality-specific ideas and practices in their work with clients, changing ideas and tactics when the approach they normally use does not "work." This often leaves the practitioner searching (mostly in vain) for the magic intervention—what "works." Moreover, while uninformed eclectic practitioners use interventions from various "schools," they remain primarily wedded to one modality. Hence, they end up confusing themselves and their clients as they search for the "right" approach, rarely looking beyond their chosen modality and therefore never actually looking outside of their self-imposed theoretical cage.

For example, an uninformed eclectic practitioner specializing in individual therapy may try a cognitive approach, a client-centered approach, a Freudian approach, or a behavioral approach, etc. A family therapy specialist may use a structural, strategic, or solution-focused approach. However, in the end, little changes. These practitioners still believe that their clients need individual or family treatment. They rarely consider potentially useful ideas and tactics taken from different modalities that could be used instead of, or in combination with, an individual or family approach, mostly because they base treatment decisions on their chosen modality.

While informed eclecticism is the goal, most find it difficult to find consistency when trying to work from a variety of models at the same time. The informed eclectic practitioners, through experience and empirical evidence, have a unifying approach that serves as the basis for using different models or methods. What is important, according to clinical outcome research, is the consistency of approach in helping facilitate successful client outcome (Gaston, 1990; Miller & Rollnick, 2002; Harper & Lantz, 1996). Trying to be eclectic makes consistency (and treatment success) quite difficult.

What uninformed eclecticism lacks is the framework needed to gain a holistic and comprehensive understanding of the client in the context of their life, history, and multiple environments that leads naturally to culturally consistent treatment and intervention decisions. AMS, as it is described here, provides such a framework. It is holistic, integrative, ecological, and based in the latest empirical evidence. It is an inclusive framework that bases treatment decisions on a multi-systemic assessment of specific client history and culture. It is designed, whenever possible, to capitalize on client strengths, be consistent with culturally specific help-seeking behavior, and utilize existing or formulated community-based and/or natural support systems in the client's environment.

Defining Multi-Systemic Client Information

In this section we specifically discuss the different dimensions that comprise AMS practice. This is a general look at what constitutes multi-systemic client life information. There are six levels of information that, when integrated into a life history of clients, demonstrate how multiple theories, models, and approaches can be applied to better understand, assess, and treat clients or client-systems. Generally, the six dimensions (biological, psychological/emotional, family, religious/spiritual/existential, social/environmental, and macro) encompass range of information needed to complete a comprehensive multi-systemic assessment, treatment, and intervention plan with client-systems of all sizes and configurations.

1. Biological Dimension

AMS practitioners need to understand what some have called the "mind-body connection," or the links between social/emotional, behavioral, and potential biological or genetic issues that may be, at least in part, driving the problems presented by clients in practice. As scientific evidence mounts regarding the biological and genetic sources of personal troubles (e.g., some mental illness), it grows imperative for well-trained AMS practitioners to apply this knowledge in everyday work with clients (Ginsberg, Nackerud, & Larrison, 2004). The responsibility for understanding biology and physical health goes well beyond those working in direct health care practice settings (e.g., hospital, HIV, or hospice practice settings). Issues pertaining to physical health confront practitioners in all practice settings.

For example, practitioners working in mental health settings are confronted daily with issues pertaining to human biology, the sources and determinants of mental illness, differential uses of psychotropic medication, and often the role played in client behavior by proper nutrition, appropriate health care, and even physical rest. In foster care and/or family preservation, practitioners also confront the effects of parental abuses (e.g., fetal alcohol syndrome [FAS]), medication management, and child/adolescent physical and biological development issues.

Beyond learning about the potential biological or physical determinants of various client troubles, having a keen understanding of the potential physical and health risks associated with various behaviors and/or lifestyles places practitioners in the position of intervening to save lives. For example, practitioners working with substance-abusing or chemically dependent clients must understand drug pharmacology—especially drug mixing—to predict potentially life-threatening physical withdrawal effects and/or to prevent intentional or unintentional harm caused by drug overdose (Johnson, 2004).

AMS requires that practitioners keep current with the latest information about human biology, development, genetics, and potential associated health risks facing clients and client-systems in practice. With that knowledge, practitioners can include this information during client assessment, treatment planning, and intervention strategies. It also requires practitioners to know the limits of professional responsibility. That is, social workers are not physicians and should never offer medical advice or guidance that is not supported by properly trained physicians. Therefore, AMS practitioners utilize the appropriate medical professionals as part of assessment, planning, and intervention processes with all clients.

2. Psychological/Emotional Dimension

AMS practitioners need a working knowledge of the ways that psychological and emotional functioning are intertwined with clients' problems and strengths, how issues from this dimension contribute to the way their client or client-system interacts with self and others in their environment, and how their environments influence their psychological and emotional functioning. There are several important skill sets that practitioners must develop to consider issues in this dimension. First, being able to recognize potential problems through a mental screening examination is a skill necessary to all practitioners. Also, having a keen understanding of the *Diagnostic and Statistical Manual of Mental Disorders* (DSM) (American Psychiatric Association, 2000), including the multi-axial diagnostic process, and recognition of the limits of this tool in the overall multi-systemic assessment process are instrumental. Especially critical is the ability to recognize co-occurring disorders (Johnson, 2004). It is also valuable to learn the Person-in-Environment (PIE) assessment system (Karls & Wandrei, 1994a, 1994b), a diagnostic model developed specifically for social workers to incorporate environmental influences.

In addition to understanding how psychology and emotion affect client mood and behavior, AMS practitioners also know how to employ different theories and models used for treating psychological and emotional functioning problems in the context of clients' multi-systemic assessment and treatment plan. This includes methods of treating individuals, families, and groups. Depending on clients' multi-systemic assessment, each of these modalities or some combination of modalities is appropriate for people with problems in this dimension.

3. Family Dimension

The family is the primary source of socialization, modeling, and nurturing of children. Hence, the family system has a significant impact on people's behavior, and people's behavior has significant impact on the health and well-being of their family system (Johnson, 2004). By integrating a family systems perspective into AMS, practitioners will often be able to make sense of behavior attitudes, beliefs, and values that would otherwise be difficult to understand or explain.

For our purposes, a family is defined as a group of people—regardless of their actual blood or legal relationship—whom clients consider to be members of their family (Johnson, 2004). This definition is designed to privilege clients' perceptions and subjective construction of reality and avoid disagreements over who is or is not in someone's family. So, if a client refers to a neighbor as "Uncle Joe," then that perception represents their reality. What good would it do to argue otherwise? Just as in client engagement discussed earlier, AMS practitioners seek to understand and embrace their clients' unique definition of family rather than imposing a rigid standard that may not fit their perceived reality. This is especially important when dealing with gay and lesbian clients. The law may not recognize gay or lesbian marriage, but AMS practitioners must, if that is the nature of the clients' relationship and consistent with their belief system.

It is important to have a working knowledge of different theories and approaches to assessing and treating families and couples, as well as the ability to construct three-generation genograms to help conceptualize family systems and characterize the relationships that exist within the family system and between the family and its environment. Family treatment requires unique skills, specialized post-graduate training, and regular supervision before practitioners can master the methods and call themselves a "family therapist." However, the journey toward mastery is well worth it. Family treatment can be among the most effective and meaningful treatment modalities, whether used in conjunction with other modalities (individual and/or group treatment) or as the primary treatment method.

4. Religious/Spiritual/Existential Dimension

Practitioners, students, and social work educators are often wary of exploring issues related to religion and spirituality in practice or the classroom. While there are exceptions, this important dimension often goes unexamined. Exploring people's religious beliefs and/or the tenets of their faith, even if they do not appear to have faith in spiritual beliefs, as they pertain to people's subjective definition of self in relation to the world is an important part of AMS practice.

How clients view themselves in relation to others and their world provides an interesting window into the inner workings of their individual interpretation of culture. The extent that clients have internalized messages (positive, negative, and/or neutral) about their behavior from their faith community or personal spiritual belief systems can lead to an understanding of why people approach their lives and others in the ways they do. Moreover, much can be learned, based on these beliefs, about people's belief in the potential for change, how change occurs, and who is best suited to help in that change process (if anyone at all), especially as it relates to the many moral and religious messages conveyed about people with problems.

Examination of this dimension goes beyond discovering which church or synagogue clients attend. It is designed to learn how and by what means clients define themselves and their lives in their world, what tenets they use to justify their lives, and how these tenets either support their current lives or can be used to help lead them toward change. There is much to be learned about client culture, how people interpret their culture in daily life, and how they view their life in their personal context from an examination of their religious or spiritual beliefs.

Moreover, religious and spiritual belief systems can also be a source of strength and support when considered in treatment plans. For example, while many clients may benefit from attendance at a community support group (e.g., Alcoholics Anonymous, Overeaters Anonymous) or professional treatment, some will benefit even more from participation in groups and events through local houses of worship. In our experience, many clients unable to succeed in professional treatment or support groups found success through a connection or reconnection with organizations that share their faith, whatever that faith may be.

5. Social/Environmental Dimension

Beyond the individual and family, AMS practitioners look to the client's community, including the physical environment, for important clues to help with engagement, assessment, and intervention planning. People live in communities comprised of three different types: (1) location (neighborhoods, cities, and rural or urban villages), (2) identification (religion, culture, race, etc.), and (3) affiliation (group memberships, subcultures, professional, political/ ideological groups, etc.). There are six subdimensions that comprise the social/environmental dimension and incorporate the three types of communities listed above (Johnson, 2004). They are:

1. Local community.   This includes learning about physical environment, living conditions, a person's fit within their community and neighborhoods, where and how people live on a daily basis, and how they believe they are treated and/or accepted by community members and the community's power structure (e.g., the police).

2. Cultural context.   This includes learning about clients' larger culture, their individual interpretation of culture, and how it drives or influences their daily life. Also included here is an exploration of histories of oppression and discrimination (individual, family, and community) and a client's subcultural group membership (e.g., drug culture, gang culture).

3. Social class.   Often overlooked by practitioners, "information about people's social class is directly related to information about their families, the goodness-of-fit between the person and environment, and the strengths, resources, and/or barriers in their communities" (Johnson, 2004, p. 226). Some believe that no other demographic factor explains so extensively the differences between people and/or groups (Lipsitz, 1997; Davis & Proctor, 1989). Social class represents a combination of income, education, occupation, prestige, and community. It encompasses how these factors affect people's relative wealth and access to power and opportunity (Johnson, 2004).

4. Social/relational. Human beings are social creatures who define themselves in relation to others (Johnson, 2004). Therefore, it is necessary to know something about people's ability to relate to others in their social environment. This investigation includes loved ones, friends, peers, supervisors, teachers, and others that they relate to in their daily life.

5. Legal history and involvement. Obviously, this subdimension includes information about involvement with the legal system by the client, family members, and friends and peers. More than recording a simple demographic history, seek to discover their feelings, attitudes, and beliefs about themselves, their place in the world, and how their brushes with the law fit into or influence their worldview.

6. Community resources. Investigate the nature and availability of organizational support, including the role of social service organizations, politics, and your presence as a social worker in a client's life. For example, can clients find a program to serve their needs, or what does seeing a social worker mean within their community or culture? What are the conditions of the schools and the influence of churches, neighborhood associations, and block clubs? More importantly, what is the prevailing culture of the local environment? Are neighbors supportive or afraid of each other, and can a client expect to reside in the present situation and receive the support needed to change?

Be sure to include the professional helping system in this subdimension. Practitioners, their agencies, and the policies that assist or impede the professional helping process join with client-systems as part of the overall system in treatment. In other words, we must consider ourselves as part of the system—we do not stand outside in objective observation. This includes practitioner qualities and styles, agency policies, broader policies related to specific populations, and reimbursement policies, including managed care. All of these factors routinely influence the extent to which clients receive help, how clients are perceived in the helping system, and, in the case of reimbursement policies, the method of treatment clients are eligible to receive regardless of how their multi-systemic assessment turns out.

Familiarity with various theories and models of community provides the key to understanding the role of the social, physical, political, and economic environment in an individual's life. Community models look at the broader environment and its impact on people. Clients or client-systems with issues located in this dimension often respond well to group and family treatment methods. Occasionally, practitioners will be required to intervene at the local neighborhood or community level through organizing efforts and/or personal or political advocacy. For example:

> I (Johnson) was treating a client in individual and occasional family treatment when it was discovered that the daughter had been molested by a neighbor. The parents had not reported the molestation. I soon learned that this neighbor was rumored to have molested several young girls in the neighborhood and that nobody was willing to

report the molestations. I urged my client to organize a neighborhood meeting of all involved parents at her home. I served as the group facilitator for an intense meeting that ultimately built the community support needed to involve law enforcement. Within days, all of the parents in this group met with law enforcement. The perpetrator was arrested, convicted, and sentenced to life imprisonment.

6. Macro Dimension

AMS practitioners do not stop looking for relevant client information at the local level. They also look for clues in the way that macro issues influence clients, their problems, and potential for change. Knowledge of various laws (local, state, and national) is critical, as is an understanding of how various social policies are interpreted and enforced in a particular client's life. For example, AMS requires an understanding of how child welfare policies affect the life of a chemically dependent mother, how health care policy affects a family's decisions about seeking medical treatment for their children, or how local standards of hygiene or cleanliness affect a family's status and acceptance in their community.

Issues to consider at this level also include public sentiment, stereotypes, and mechanisms of oppression that play a significant role in the lives of people who are not Caucasian, male, middle-class (or more affluent) citizens. Racism, classism, homophobia, and sexism, to name a few, are real threats to people who are attempting to live a "normal" life. An AMS practitioner must understand this reality and learn from clients what their individual perceptions are of these mechanisms and how they affect their problems and potential for change. The macro dimension involves issues such as housing, employment, and public support, along with the dynamics of the criminal justice system. For example, if clients have been arrested for domestic violence, what is the chance they will get fair and just legal representation? If they have been convicted and served jail or prison sentences, what are the chances they will have a reasonable chance of finding sufficient employment upon release?

These issues can be addressed in individual, family, or group treatment. Often, group treatment is an effective way to address issues clients struggle with at the macro level. Group treatment provides clients a way to address these issues in the context of mutual social support and a sense of belonging, helping them realize that they are not alone in their struggles (Yalom, 1995). AMS practitioners also recognize the need for political advocacy and community-organizing methods for clients who present with consistent struggles with issues at the macro level.

Summary

The hallmark of AMS is its reliance on and integration of multi-systemic client information into one comprehensive assessment, treatment, and intervention plan. It incorporates knowledge, skills, and values from multiple sources and relies on various sources of knowledge to paint a holistic picture of people's lives, struggles, strengths and resources, and potential for change. Practitioners need a current working knowledge of human behavior, social systems theories, the latest social research and practice evaluation results, and the impact of public laws and policies, as well as the skills and abilities to plan and implement treatment approaches as needed, in a manner consistent with our definition of informed eclecticism.

Many students new to AMS start out confused because the requirements seem so diverse and complicated. However, as you will see in the case presentations to follow, an organized and efficient practitioner who has learned to think and act multi-systemically can gather large amounts of critically important information about a client in a relatively short period. For this to happen, you must have a deep understanding of various theories, models, and practice approaches that address the various systemic levels considered and be willing to accept that no single model is completely right or wrong. It is always easier to latch on to one model and "go with it." However, the goal of practice is not to be correct or to promote your own ease and comfort, but to develop an assessment and treatment plan that is right for each client, whether or not you would ever use it in your own life. Social work practice is not about the social worker, but the client. It is important never to lose sight of this fact.

Bibliography

American Psychiatric Association. (2000). *Diagnostic and statistical manual of mental disorders* (4th ed.-TR). Washington, DC: Author.

Appleby, G. A. (2001). Dynamics of oppression and discrimination. In G. A. Appleby, E. Colon, & J. Hamilton (Eds.), *Diversity, oppression, and social functioning: Person-in-environment assessment and intervention.* Boston: Allyn and Bacon.

Best, S., & Kellner, D. (1991). *Postmodern theory: Critical interrogations.* New York: Guilford Press.

Cournoyer, B. R. (2004). *The evidence-based social work skills book.* Boston: Allyn and Bacon.

Cox, E. O., & Parsons, R. J. (1994). *Empowerment-oriented social work practice with the elderly.* Pacific Grove, CA: Brooks/Cole.

Davis, L. E., & Proctor, E. K. (1989). *Race, gender, and class: Guidelines for practice with individuals, families, and groups.* Englewood Cliffs, NJ: Prentice-Hall.

Derezotes, D. S. (2000). *Advanced generalist social work practice.* Thousand Oaks, CA: Sage.

Fong, R. (2001). Culturally competent social work practice: Past and present. In R. Fong & S. Furuto (Eds.), *Culturally competent practice: Skills, interventions, and evaluations.* Boston: Allyn and Bacon.

Freire, P. (1993). *Pedagogy of the oppressed.* New York: Continuum.

Gambrill, E. (1997). *Social work practice: A critical thinker's guide.* New York: Oxford University Press.

Gambrill, E. (1990). *Critical thinking in clinical practice.* San Francisco: Jossey-Bass.

Gaston, L. (1990). The concept of the alliance and its role in psychotherapy: Theoretical and empirical considerations. *Psychotherapy, 27,* 143–153.

Geertz, C. (1973). *The interpretation of cultures.* New York: Basic Books.

Germain, C. B., & Gitterman, A. (1980). *The ecological model of social work practice.* New York: Columbia University Press.

Germain, C. B., & Gitterman, A. (1996). *The life model of social work practice* (2nd ed.). New York: Columbia University Press.

Gibbs, L. E. (2003). *Evidence-based practice for the helping professions: A practical guide with integrated multimedia.* Pacific Grove, CA: Brooks/Cole.

Ginsberg, L., Nackerud, L., & Larrison, C. R. (2004). *Human biology for social workers: Development, ecology, genetics, and health.* Boston: Allyn and Bacon.

GlenMaye, L. (1998). Empowerment of women. In L. M. Gutierrez, R. J. Parsons, & E. O. Cox (eds.), *Empowerment in social work practice: A sourcebook.* Pacific Grove, CA: Brooks/Cole.

Gordon, J. U. (1993). A culturally specific approach to ethnic minority young adults. In E. M. Freeman (Ed.), *Substance abuse treatment: A family systems perspective.* Newbury Park, CA: Sage.

Greif, G. L. (1986). The ecosystems perspective "meets the press." *Social Work, 31,* 225–226.

Harper, K. V., & Lantz, J. (1996). *Cross-cultural practice: Social work practice with diverse populations.* Chicago: Lyceum Books.

Johnson, J. L. (2004). *Fundamentals of substance abuse practice.* Pacific Grove, CA: Brooks/Cole.

Johnson, J. L. (2000). *Crossing borders—confronting history: Intercultural adjustment in a post-Cold War world.* Lanham, MD: University Press of America.

Karls, J., & Wandrei, K. (1994a). *Person-in-environment system: The PIE classification system for functioning problems.* Washington, DC: NASW.

Karls, J., & Wandrei, K. (1994b). *PIE manual: Person-in-environment system: The PIE classification system for social functioning.* Washington, DC: NASW.

Kozol, J. (1991). *Savage inequalities: Children in America's schools.* New York: Crown Publishers.

Leigh, J. W. (1998). *Communicating for cultural competence.* Boston: Allyn and Bacon.

Lipsitz, G. (1997). Class and class consciousness: Teaching about social class in public universities. In A. Kumar (Ed.), *Class issues.* New York: New York University Press.

Longres, J. F. (2000). *Human behavior in the social environment* (3rd ed.). Itasca, IL: F.E. Peacock.

Lum, D. (1999). *Culturally competent practice.* Pacific Grove, CA: Brooks/Cole.

McLaren, P. (1995). *Critical pedagogy and predatory culture: Oppositional politics in a postmodern era.* London: Routledge.

Miley, K. K., O'Melia, M., & DuBois, B. (2004). *Generalist social work practice: An empowerment approach.* Boston: Allyn and Bacon.

Miller, W. R., & Rollnick, S. (2002). *Motivational interviewing: Preparing people to change addictive behavior* (2nd ed.). New York: Guilford Press.

Mills, C. W. (1959). *The sociological imagination.* New York: Oxford University Press.

Parsons, R. J., Gutierrez, L. M., & Cox, E. O. (1998). A model for empowerment practice. In L. M. Gutierrez, R. J. Parsons, & E. O. Cox (eds.), *Empowerment in social work practice: A sourcebook.* Pacific Grove, CA: Brooks/Cole.

Pinderhughes, E. (1989). *Understanding race, ethnicity, and power.* New York: Free Press.

Popper, K. R. (1994). *The myth of the framework: In defense of science and rationality.* Edited by M. A. Notturno. New York: Routledge.

Saleebey, D. (2002). *The strengths perspective in social work practice* (3rd ed.). Boston: Allyn and Bacon.

Smelser, N. J. (1992). Culture: Coherent or incoherent. In R. Munch & N. J. Smelser (Eds.), *Theory of culture.* Berkeley, CA: University of California Press.

Timberlake, E. M., Farber, M. Z., & Sabatino, C. A. (2002). *The general method of social work practice: McMahon's generalist perspective* (4th ed.). Boston: Allyn and Bacon.

van Wormer, K., & Davis, D. R. (2003). *Addiction treatment: A strengths perspective.* Pacific Grove, CA: Brooks/Cole.

Yalom, I. (1995). *The theory and practice of group psychotherapy* (4th ed.). New York: Basic Books.

2

Mikki's Story

Carolyn Jumpper-Black & Sandra Shelly

Introduction

I once worked in a shelter for battered women and their children. The shelter was located in a Midwestern, urban area and was funded through donations and grants. The staff consisted of a director, two MSW social workers, three paraprofessionals, and a paralegal. Shelter staff provided twenty-four-hour care and offered a crisis line. It also provided childcare, support groups, legal advocacy, children's support groups, drug and alcohol counseling, job coaching, and housing. Mikki came to the shelter one day, referred to us by a hospital social worker. The hospital social worker provided me with background information about my new client.

Mikki at Intake

Mikki was a 30-year-old, Caucasian female. She was about 5'1" tall and considerably overweight. She was admitted to a medical-surgical unit of the hospital for complications from intestinal bypass surgery she underwent approximately six months earlier. At the time of her surgery, Mikki was morbidly obese (over 300 pounds). It was a last ditch effort to lose weight because of seriousness of the surgical procedure and its many side effects. Mikki complained about weakness, dizziness, frequent diarrhea, emesis, and a high fever. In addition, her eyes and skin had a yellowish color, usual complications of the surgery. Laboratory tests revealed that she had an infection, her liver functions and electrolytes were outside normal ranges, and she was dehydrated. Prior to surgery, Mikki weighed 320 pounds. When I met her, she weighed 220 pounds.

After a week in the hospital, Mikki's medical condition improved, making her ready for discharge. Her laboratory results were normal and she could perform her daily activities. She was limited to climbing stairs twice per day. The morning of discharge, Mikki revealed to the nurse that she was essentially homeless. The nurse called the hospital social worker to make an emergency placement, and she referred Mikki to our shelter. That's when Mikki and I met for the first time.

According to the hospital social worker, Mikki was evasive about her past. She provided little family history. Her father died when she was a teenager; her mother currently lived in the city, but Mikki seldom saw her. She also had one brother, although they had not spoken in several years. Her brother also lived in the city, but she did not know where. Mikki was married. However, she and her husband separated about nine months earlier. She refused to provide details about why they separated. Mikki also said that they had no children.

After separating from her husband, Mikki lived with a female friend while recuperating from surgery. Mikki said that one night they went to a free concert, where she met her current boyfriend. She and Don exchanged telephone numbers, and he began calling her. Mikki's friend disliked Don because he was from a "different racial persuasion." Within three weeks of meeting, Mikki moved in with the man.

Mikki said that Don often called her a "fat bitch" and "got physical" sometimes. However, she refused to provide details about her exact definition of "got physical." Just before she returned to the hospital, Mikki resumed living with her friend. However, Mikki said that she could not return to her friend's house and did not want to go back with her boyfriend. When pressed for the reason she could not return to her friend's house, she claimed, "There's not enough room; she has three kids."

Falling Through the Cracks

I was on intake when the hospital social worker called the shelter. I advised the social worker that the shelter was not a nursing facility; we could not provide medical care, nor did we have staff trained to provide that care. The social worker was tenacious, assuring me that Mikki could take care of herself. I reminded her that the client had mobility limitations. The shelter did not have an elevator. The bedrooms were on the second floor and the main dining and group meeting areas were on the first floor. The social worker stated that Mikki had done well in physical therapy, and if she limited stair climbing to coming down for meals and going up to bed, she should fare well. The client was scheduled for follow-up appointments in the gastrointestinal clinic and outpatient physical therapy.

I advised the hospital social worker that I could not unilaterally make the decision. The shelter director, team members, and, perhaps, legal counsel must be consulted. The shelter director was out of the facility and a decision would wait until the next day. That evening, I reached the director and legal counsel. Both were reluctant to accept the client because shelter staff could not address her medical needs.

I pointed out that our agency's mission was to help women escape the web of domestic violence. Perhaps, I continued, with some minor adjustments we could accommodate Mikki. The director and legal counsel agreed to accept her only if the hospital would send a copy of the client's discharge instructions and accept her back if she became medically distressed. In addition, the hospital social worker would have to arrange transportation for medical appointments.

The next morning, the shelter director and I met with the team. We decided to accept Mikki on a "trial" basis, and I was assigned as her primary therapist. I contacted the hospital social worker and arranged for her admission to our shelter. Finally, at about eight o'clock that evening, workers from a city social services agency transported Mikki to the shelter. We had an agreement with this agency to provide transportation for women to the shelter to protect the anonymity of the shelter's location. Mikki arrived at the shelter looking tired, scared, and confused.

The difficult time we had gaining Mikki's admission to the shelter system illustrates the shortsightedness of shelter planners and administrators. They assumed that women needing domestic violence protection would all be healthy women. While the women might have sustained injuries from their abusive partners, they would not have mobility limitations or chronic medical conditions that posed continuous challenges for them.

Mikki could have easily fallen through the cracks of the service delivery system. Neither the health care system nor the shelter system was designed to address her needs. Moreover, she seemed to lack an adequate network of family and friends to help her, and by her presentation at the shelter, she seemed to lack the internal resources to advocate on her own behalf. Only because the hospital social worker and I advocated for her, could Mikki enter the shelter system.

Questions

Domestic violence cases frequently appear on caseloads wherever social workers and other helping professionals practice. Therefore, it will serve you well to understand the problems and their recommended treatments.

1. Explore the professional literature, best practice evidence, and multi-disciplinary literature about domestic violence. Explain the depth and breadth of the problem, examining all facets of it pertaining to populations, demographics and family structures and in the context of gender and patriarchy.

2. Pertaining specifically to practice, what models, methods, or theories do the literature recommend for work in domestic violence? Examine the extent to which treatments focus on survivors versus batterers. What are the latest program models and initiatives aimed at domestic violence treatment?

3. Through reading and dialogue, explore domestic violence in the context of culture. Specifically, in recent years have opinions changed about either survivors or batterers? Explain and defend your position.

4. Pertaining specifically to this case, what hunches or initial ideas do you have about this case? If you were the practitioner, what direction or approach would you take with Mikki during your first individual session? Make a list of potential issues and strengths, and maintain this list as you discover new information about the case.

Battered Women: Theoretical Considerations

Many of the theories and models used to work with battered women do not consider how clients change or reconstruct their lives over time. It often frustrates practitioners when battered women do not adhere to treatment suggestions and recommendations. Many perceive this as "resistance" or lack of progress. This can lead to blaming battered women for their situations.

Principles from constructivist theory and the transtheoretical change model hold promise as intervention tools with battered women, helping them to use their resources to devise and implement their own solutions. Validating battered women's definitions of reality and acknowledging their current stage of change help operationalize client-centered practice and facilitate a sense of empowerment.

The Need for Alternative Paradigms

Battered women leave and return to physically violent relationships several times before permanently leaving (Griffing et al., 2002; Stackman, 1997; Simerly, 1996; Rusbult & Martz, 1995). Rusbult and Martz (1995) found that a sense of commitment to the relationship was a salient factor in determining whether women returned to their abusive partners. Women with fewer economic choices, who were married, and who had survived less severe physical abuse tend to remain in abusive relationships.

A more recent study (Griffing et al., 2002) examined women's self-identified reasons for returning to abusive partners. Out of ninety female residents of an urban domestic violence shelter, almost 67 percent reported previously leaving their partners and then returning to them. Compared to women leaving for the first time, women with histories of relationship separations were significantly more likely to return because of their continued attachment to the partners. Leaving and returning from abusive relationships are part of the domestic violence syndrome. Some women permanently leave abusive relationships, some continue to leave and return, and others choose to stay in their tumultuous relationships with abusive partners (Busch, 2001; Lerner & Kennedy, 2000; Peled, Eisikovits, Enosh, & Winstok, 2000).

In most cases, practitioners usually want or require battered women to leave their partners and file legal charges. This generic intervention often discounts what battered women want and define as helpful (Black, 2001; Smith, 2001; Davies,

Lyon, & Monti, 1998; Mills, 1998). There are many reasons battered women remain with abusive partners, for example, financial dependence on partner, concern for children, pressure from family, fear of retaliation from partner, and emotional attachment to partner (Barnett, 2001; Barnett, 2000; Chornesky, 2000). Practitioners are wrong to believe that leaving equates with a "happy ever after ending."

Over the years, research has demonstrated that for some women, leaving places them at greater risk of harm from their partners than staying with them (Mills, 1998; Morton, Runyan, Moracco, & Butts, 1998; Walker & Meloy, 1998). According to one study (Morton et al., 1998), separating from an abusive partner contributed to 41 percent of female homicides. In homicides that included domestic violence, nearly half of the victims had previously sought protection from the perpetrator in the form of arrest warrants, restraining orders, or intervention by law enforcement officers. Although research belies the prescription of leaving and filing charges, most domestic violence policies and programs assume that this intervention is appropriate for every battered woman (Smith, 2001; Barnett; 2000; Bennett, Goodman, & Dutton; 1999; Mills, 1999; Mills, 1998; Baker, 1997).

Battered women might not vocalize their displeasure with this generic prescription, but their behavior indicates otherwise. They often do not call the police, file charges, or prosecute their partners. Moreover, they often return to their partners after a short time in a shelter or drop out of counseling altogether (Bennett et al., 1999; Fleury, Sullivan & Bybee, 1998; Mills, 1998; Erez & Belknap, 1998). Bennett et al. (1999) discovered that battered women were reluctant to follow through with criminal prosecution because of the complex, confusing, and frustrating court systems. Furthermore, between the partner's arrest and the resolution of the court case, many women live in fear and believe that the legal system cannot protect them. Hence, many women leave the social service system rather than their partners. To them, it is a safer alternative, given the narrow range of choices offered by practitioners and domestic violence programs.

For practitioners, these problems frequently lead to negative attitudes about battered women and burnout. Frustrated by their client's ambivalence, practitioners often label battered women as dependent, pathological, and masochistic, placing the onus of victimization on the women (Busch, 2001; Dekel & Peled, 2000; Brown & O'Brien, 1998). Few choices and callous attitudes further isolate and alienate these women. Distrustful of the social service delivery system, the only option remaining for many battered women is a return to their abusive partners, often without community support or membership. According to Walzer, "to be without membership is to be in a condition of infinite danger" (cited in Saleebey, 1997, p. 9).

Constructivist Theory

A primary assumption of constructivist theory is that people define reality based on their experience and perception of lived experience. Therefore, people's definition of reality is a subjective mental process rather than an objective external "truth."

People know their world through their experience of their world (Peled et al., 2000; Eisikovits & Buchbinder, 1999; Gallant, 1993). In other words, there is not one but multiple realities that exist in the mind of the beholders. Therefore, in theory, there is no hierarchy of realities. One reality is no better than another is. A client's construct of reality has just as much legitimacy as that of the therapist (see Chapter 1 for more information).

As practitioners, constructivists examine client perceptions and beliefs. There are no rigid norms or standards of normal or pathological behavior. The salient task for the practitioner is to understand how clients make sense of themselves and their worlds. However, client views of their worlds can be a barrier to finding alternative solutions and/or embroil them in a web of conflict where the problem takes on a life of its own and limits their repertoire of responses (Gallant, 1993).

To help clients disentangle from their web of conflict, practitioners work collaboratively with clients. The client, not the practitioner, is the expert on their personal reality. Together, clients and practitioners explore alternative realities to expand the repertoire of responses to the problem (Gallant, 1993; de Shazer; 1988). As people begin thinking differently, they feel differently, and eventually behave differently. Therefore, they construct an alternative reality for themselves. Thinking and behaving differently are essential elements of the change process.

Battered Women's Constructs

In two recent studies, Eisikovits and Buchbinder (1999) and Baker (1997) illustrate how battered women construct realities that are often in conflict with a society that endorses leaving and staying away from their abusive partners as the only acceptable response to domestic violence. Often, this construct is the antithesis of many battered women's worldviews and goals for their relationships with their partners.

Baker (1997) found that many women resisted what she termed the dominant cultural script because it was too narrow and lacked adequate institutional support. Women resisted by staying with or returning to their partners; ignoring or lifting restraining orders; and refusing to call or not cooperating with the police. Fear and harassment from their partners, concerns about children and finances, and emotional connections to their partners were major reasons why women did not adhere to the dominant cultural script.

Women's decisions were not capricious but based on how they viewed their options and their negative perceptions about treatment agencies. Baker called the system disempowering to battered women. It dictates certain behaviors but fails to provide the necessary support and resources to implement those behaviors. Baker (1997) further advocated for programs and policies for battered women who chose to stay with their partners and for more programs geared toward their violent partners. That is, Baker (1997) recommended liberating battered women from the unilateral responsibility of stopping physical violence in their lives.

The study by Eisikovits and Buchbinder (1999) explored battered women's perception of violent events by examining how women used language in the form of metaphors. The researchers learned that language has a surface structure, the description of the overt content of the words spoken, and a deep structure, the interpretation, meaning, and emotions embedded in their words. Metaphors become the bridge between the two structures.

For example, when talking about their partners' violent outbursts, women often used the metaphor of "a volcanic eruption." Most women knew the "early warning signs" and believed they could somehow control the eruption by controlling their words (e.g., not verbally responding to their partners, talking softly, and/or not saying insulting things to their partners). Many women accepted the man's belief that violence was beyond his control. Thus, the violence became an entity separate and distinct from the person. By accepting this construct, women created a reality for themselves where they had unilateral responsibility for controlling violence in the relationship. Not only did they have to recognize the early warning signs of violence, they also had to control their responses to control their partners' violence. Men assumed no responsibility for the violence since they could not control themselves (Eisikovits & Buchbinder, 1999).

Women continued to believe the separation by talking about the good side of their partner, suggesting that only they knew the nonviolent side of him. Women believe they can love that good side because it struggled valiantly with the "erupting volcano." Women constructed their realities in a way that made it possible to continue living with their abuser, without needing outside help. The researcher contended that women needed to learn an alternative reality where the man and violence fused. When this happened, they would make their abuser responsible for his behavior, making it nearly impossible to stay in the relationship (Eisikovits & Buchbinder, 1999).

Transtheoretical Change Theory

An individual's view of reality and readiness for change are closely related. Change is not an instantaneous phenomenon but a process. Researchers have uncovered stages that individuals navigate before permanent change occurs. As individuals navigate the stages of change, their definition of reality also changes (Prochaska, 1996; McConnaughy, DiClemente, Proschaska & Velicer, 1989; McConnaughy, Proschaska, & Velicer, 1983).

Research by Proschaska (1996) and McConnaughy et al. (1989, 1983) operationalized the change process. Augmenting the work of earlier researchers on change, these researchers developed a transtheoretical change model that identified six stages of behavioral change. The stages of change include:

1. Precontemplation.   In this stage, clients enter treatment with the wish to change others or the environment, often being coerced into treatment by the courts or significant others. These clients are not choosing to change themselves and have not considered, even for a moment, the possibility that they have problems.

2. Contemplation.   In this stage, clients are aware of problems and are interested in determining whether the problems are resolvable and whether therapy could be helpful to them.

3. Preparation.   In this stage, clients have attempted to make a clear resolution of the parameters of the problem area and have made a commitment to change (Prochaska, Norcross & DiClemente, 2002).

4. Action.   In this stage, clients begin working toward change and seek help implementing action strategies. Specific techniques geared to this stage of change may bring about the desired results.

5. Maintenance.   In this stage, clients have changed but seek further help to consolidate their previous gains. They are beginning to replace problem behaviors with healthier choices (McConnaughy et al., 1989, p. 494).

6. Termination.   In this stage, clients have reached their goals and have confidence that (s)he can cope without fear of relapse. The client anticipates exiting the cycle of change and winning the struggle.

Additionally, there are "systematic relationships among the stages and the processes of change" (Prochaska et al., 2002, p. 53). That is, interventions need to be congruent with people's current stage of change. According to Prochaska et al., (2002) "effective self-change depends on doing the right things at the right times" (p. 59). Practitioners must apply different interventions at different change stages. Client resistance increases if an intervention is incompatible with the client's stage and when spouses or other family members are in different stages of change.

Moreover, client dropout also relates to people's stage of change (McConnaughy et al., 1983). While 45 percent of clients drop out after a few sessions, practitioners often label these clients unmotivated, resistant, or not ready for therapy. Practitioners often act as if dropouts are rare, when in fact, high dropout rates are common (Hadley, Short, Legin & Zook, 1995; Pagelow, 1981). Prochaska et al. (2002) demonstrated that most people quit therapy when it fails to meet their stage-specific needs, and not because of a lack of motivation. Additionally, clients fluctuate between stages (McConnaughy et al., 1989). That is, the stages are not discrete and successive. Clients often present between stages or move back and forth among the stages. Moreover, there are no distinct time limits for clients to remain in a particular stage.

The authors initially used this model for clients struggling with addictive behaviors, such as smoking or drinking. However, others used it with other problems, including dietary modification, gambling, and environmental safety issues (DiClemente & Velasques, 2002; DiClemente, Story & Murray, 2000; Glanz et al., 1994; Marcus, Rossie, Selby, Niaura & Abrams, 1992; DiClemente &

Prochaska, 1985). Although the target behaviors differed, the structure of the change process appeared the same. Individuals moved from being unaware or unwilling to change to considering the possibility of change to preparing to make changes, and finally, to taking action and sustaining change.

Integrating Theory and Practice

In recent years, researchers have begun examining the efficacy of the transtheoretical change model in work with battered women (Burke, Gielen, McDonell, O'Campo & Maman, 2001; Fever, Meade, Milstead & Resick, 1999; Wells, 1998). Most interventions directed at battered women have not considered the type of help needed, as defined by the clients, or their stage of change (Sullivan & Alexy, 2001; Bennett & Lawson, 1994; Rinfret-Raynor, Paqnet-Deeby, Larouche & Cantin, 1992). Hence, battered women become disempowered when practitioners ignore these two factors, often leaving practitioners feeling angry, frustrated, and burned out. Perhaps this is why many practitioners blame the women for their own problems, because they did not follow the dominant cultural script (Baker, 1997).

Through their stories and experiences, battered women present myriad reasons for staying with abusive partners. By acknowledging and legitimizing their stories and experiences, practitioners can understand women's realities and their stage of change. By employing principles of constructivism and transtheoretical change theory, those who work with battered women are in a better position to devise collaborative problem-solving strategies with their clients.

The experience of counseling battered women in a Midwest urban shelter illustrates how principles of constructivism and change theory work with this population. We concluded that battered women experienced a similar change process to that posited by McConnaughy et al. (1989) and Prochaska et al. (2002). We based our conclusion on practice wisdom and interviews over a ten-year period with more than 350 battered women and 100 staff persons who worked in domestic violence shelters.

The process of change for battered women is a journey from powerlessness to empowerment. It is not a linear process, rather a circular one, with clients bouncing back and forth between stages (Brown, 1997). According to Prochaska and his colleagues (2002), "completing the challenging journey from contemplation through to termination requires ongoing work, the development of a relapse prevention plan, and continuing application of the appropriate processes of change" (p. 47).

Precontemplation

At this stage, battered women are in denial. They are unsure whether abuse or battering has occurred. They are shocked, surprised, and have no desire to leave their marriage or primary relationship. Clients say things such as, "He didn't mean it," "It won't happen again," or "It was just a temper tantrum."

These women do not see the need to change. They do not want to think about the problem and often respond defensively to practitioners pressing for information or offering resources. Ironically, clients are emotionally stable in this stage. Denial and minimization provide emotional "cover." By refusing to acknowledge problems, clients can pretend that they do not exist. Denial filters out information that would require changes. During the precontemplation stage, clients may be dissatisfied and/or terrified about aspects of their life, but are often more terrified about changing. Although precarious, battered women in the precontemplation stage are balanced.

Rationalization, explanation, and intellectualization are mechanisms a battered woman might use to justify or excuse her partner's behavior. Moreover, in this stage clients defined their reality in a way that highlights a fissure between the good and bad sides of their partners. They often believe the man's violent behavior is beyond his control (Eisikovits & Buchbinder, 1999). Without help, women can remain in this stage forever. For battered women, love for their partner can override concern for their own safety (Brown, 1997).

Women often described their partner's "three faces": the fun or sensitive face, the public face, and the dark face. This is illustrated by the following case:

> M came into the shelter after receiving treatment in a local emergency room. She had sustained multiple contusions. Her boyfriend had beaten her with an oak window stick. He accused her of having romantic trysts with a sixteen-year-old neighbor boy when she took out the garbage. M talked about how good her boyfriend was with their children and how helpful he was around the house. She stated, "I know he doesn't want to be this way. . . . I don't want to see him in jail. He's supposed to be my fiancé."

Reports from clinical studies (Ryan, Plant & O'Malley, 1995; Simpson & Joe, 1993; Johnson, 1986) indicate that coerced clients come to therapy with no intention of making changes. With battered women, they may be seeking affirmation that they do not have problems and their marriages are not troubled. Furthermore, they might be looking for information about how to change or manage their abusive partners. Often, helpers approach battered women in denial with skepticism, by giving advice, using scare tactics, or with confrontation, trying to convince them of their dangerous environments. Battered women usually minimize the safety risks and rationalize any danger, thus resigning themselves to their situations.

With clients in the precontemplation stage, Connors, Donovan, and DiClemente (2001) suggested practitioners should explore the reasons why clients seek help as well as ways to move the client forward. Connors et al. (2001) posited that lack of motivation is part of the change process and suggested motivational approaches such as offering respect, careful and active listening, reflecting, summarizing, and highlighting discrepancies between goals and behaviors.

With battered women in the denial stage, practitioners should focus on safety planning and education as a precursor for future engagement. Practitioners should remember the motivational needs of the precontemplative battered woman, and should not initiate intensive action-oriented interventions with clients in this stage.

DiClemente & Velasquez (1991) suggested that practitioners use techniques to raise awareness without raising resistance, for example, values clarification exercises, information about how nonviolent relationships work, and raising awareness about the definition of their abuse experience.

According to Prochaska et al. (2002), helpers must recognize that precontemplators are powerless to change without assistance. They suggest that practitioners not push clients into action, nag them, or criticize them for their lives, behaviors, and/or beliefs. Women in the precontemplation stage are tenuous, at best. The type of help offered and their responses to the help can either aid progression to the contemplation stage or maintain the defense of their troubled relationships.

Contemplation

In the contemplation stage, clients become aware that problems exist (Prochaska et al., 2002). For the battered woman, guilt is often the dominant emotion of this stage. They believe it is their fault that they are battered. Women begin turning their feelings inward, believing that they created the problems. These women believe that if they had kept their mouth shut, had dinner on the table on time, and kept the kids quiet, their partners would not abuse them. The following vignettes demonstrate how two women struggled with guilt and denial:

> B had spent several days in intensive care because of a beating by her husband. When B was able to talk about the incident, she did not blame her husband. Instead, B stated that when she and her husband fought, she was clumsy and she fell over things.
>
> C attempted to fight back; yet, she appeared to have felt guilty about defending herself. She stated, "I know my boyfriend wouldn't have beaten me so badly if I hadn't bitten his finger."

Guilt becomes self-accusation and self-blame, resulting in low self-esteem. In this stage, women present symptoms of powerlessness, such as suicidal plans, eating disorders, sleep disorders, substance abuse, and looking for a rescuer (e.g., another partner, shelter worker, police officer, lawyer). Moreover, these women might experience symptoms of depression or other health-related problems (Chang, 1996).

Browne (1987) found that women's levels of distress, sense of danger, suicidal thoughts, and flashbacks were directly related to abuse severity. Studies revealed that victims of sexual and physical abuse by a marital partner were at risk for increased psychological damage (Browne, 1987; Pagelow, 1984). Over time, women experiencing long-term abuse become dependent, suggestible, and have trouble making decisions or carrying out long-range plans (Koss et al., 1994). Because women in the contemplation stage are often at high risk for suicide, it is imperative for shelter workers to conduct suicide risk assessments.

This is a time of great ambivalence for battered women. They are aware of their problems and know that changes must occur but fear change. Women in the contemplation stage often substitute thinking for action, fear failure, and worry about sacrificing their familiar life and partner. The following case vignette exemplifies a battered woman fearing change:

> Shelter workers became frustrated with Z. She had been to the shelter three times in the past two years. Each time she left, she returned to her abusive boyfriend. However, in group sessions with other battered women, Z displayed a high degree of introspection into their motivations and behaviors. However, she seemed incapable of making positive changes in her own behavior. When finally confronted regarding this dissonance, she replied that the thought of being alone was too "scary" for her to face.

Once women begin contemplating change, practitioners must begin helping them identify and understand which behaviors need changing. In the contemplation stage, as clients weigh the pros and cons of change, strategies that promote decision-making appear to help (Connors et al., 2001). Grimley et al. (1994) suggested consciousness raising, dramatic relief, and environmental reevaluation during this stage. Often, people in the contemplation stage are open to discussing themselves and reading self-help books.

For battered women, we found that the best intervention at this stage is referral to a support group. Women hear the experience of others and begin learning that they are not alone as abuse sufferers. They also begin admitting that their abuse was wrong. Women do not want to become battered women. Most have dreams and goals for a better life. Support groups help women to assess their dreams and define realities.

Practitioners working with battered women must know that while women in this stage might learn the causes and consequences of their problems, few will be secure and open enough to solicit input (Prochaska et al., 2002). At this stage, many battered women defend their behavior and/or their partners because they still believe that the violence is their fault.

For some battered women, the "white knight syndrome" presents a significant barrier to change. That is, clients often believe they can solve their problems by finding a rescuer or savior. Their white knight arrives in many forms, including other partners, police officers, ministers, lawyers, practitioners, or their children (as mediators and confidants). Battered women lean on someone else to solve their problems with abuse. For some, wishing, hoping, and praying for outside solutions serve as their white knight. Some women hope to salvage their relationship with their partners. Others prematurely leave their relationships, almost guaranteeing that they will find other abusive relationships.

According to Prochaska et al. (2002), premature action leads to a high failure rate. Women experiencing this phenomenon were aware of the problem. However, at this stage, few displayed the insight necessary to devise long-term solutions. Their belief in "magic" often prevents them from progressing to the preparation and action stages (Prochaska et al., 2002).

When the white knight syndrome surfaces, help clients weigh the pros and cons of their choices. If practitioners become the white knight, they should reevaluate their professional boundaries and try to engage clients with outside, social support. However, practitioners should remember that battered women do have the right of choice. Understand that the white knight phenomenon is yet another stage of change and reality reconstruction for some battered women.

Preparation

Connors et al. (2001) determined that clients do not necessarily move into action after deciding to change. Rather, they move into a stage of preparation, where they focus on planning and committing to a different way of life. This stage is transitional rather than stable, and people demonstrate both emotional and behavioral criteria for change. That is, clients in the preparation stage develop plans of action, have taken action within the past year, or made behavioral changes. However, they have not begun the work necessary to change their problems or environments (Prochaska et al., 2002). Anger often dominates battered woman during this stage. They have begun to integrate the good side of their partners with the violent side, feeling less responsibility for their partners' behavior (Eisikovits & Buchbinder, 1999). Women in this stage also begin considering life without their partners and physical violence. However, their new definitions of reality remain fragile and are often replete with revenge fantasies and plots against their abusive partners.

Not yet believing in their ability to change and needing an outlet for repressed rage, battered women often plot the death of their abusers. We have heard women tell stories about poisoning their abusers' coffee or beating them to death in their sleep. Totman (1978) and Browne (1987) concluded that battered women murder their abusers out of desperation, feeling trapped, and/or their perceived lack of alternatives. Browne and Williams (1989) theorized that the mere presence of resources to help protect women or enable them to escape violent relationships might offset the number of homicides. Nonetheless, because this stage can be volatile, practitioners should assess women's anger and discern whether they are expressing fantasies or actual murder plots.

Psychotherapy can help women in the preparation stage. In earlier stages, psychotherapy is ineffective because clients are not ready to explore their issues. In this stage, women identify who can help, how they can help, and the obstacles to receiving help. Planning should include identifying strategies needed to begin taking positive action.

According to Connors et al. (2001), practitioners should evaluate their client's skills needed to implement treatment plans and remediate skill deficits. Because battered women are used to living with partners that demand immediate gratification and with low frustration tolerances, women may reluctantly begin planning and have difficulty implementing their plans. In other words, battered women have learned to live in the moment, instead of the future. Psychotherapy can help women cope with their ambivalence. Because these women have lived in situations where they had to deny emotions, many become alienated from their actual feelings.

Psychotherapy can help women become more cognizant of their emotions by using a "feelings chart" to help clients identify and verbalize their feelings.

Grimley et al. (1994) recommended self-evaluation, self-liberation, contingency management, and a continuation of the helping relationships initiated in the contemplation stage. Successful self-changers reported that they valued the helping relationships most during the stages of contemplation, preparation, and action (Prochaska et al., 2002).

Action

Clients in the action stage have begun working on solving their problems and often seek help implementing and maintaining their change strategies. In early action stages, battered women no longer believe the abuse is their fault, but they still hope their relationship can improve and their partners miraculously change. For some women, vestiges of that hope always linger. Women in this stage may be in a new relationship or still with their abusive partners.

During this stage, client perceptions begin to change. They become aware of the serious emotional and physical consequences of living in an abusive relationship (Chang, 1996). Without question, this phase is difficult for clients because their hope for saving their relationships dies a little each day. Paradoxically, battered women might be actively engaged in changing their lives. However, many feel depressed. Many women in this stage become suicidal. Therefore, similar to the contemplation stage, practitioners should perform a suicide risk assessment during the action stage.

Practitioners often misperceive or discount the seriousness of this stage. They are often elated that their clients have "seen the light." However, they can easily forget that women are also reconstructing their realities and redefining themselves. Additionally, women are mourning the loss of their former identity and life. Hence, clients are simultaneously mourning the loss of their partners and the loss of their dreams about how the relationships "should" have been (Para, Arkowitz, Hannah & Vasquez, 1995; Smith & Gray, 1995; Katz & Florian, 1986). For example,

> An outreach worker had followed P since she had left the shelter. P's divorce was to be final in about a week. The outreach worker was somewhat puzzled by P's depressed affect. She asked P why she was not happy that she was finally getting out of an abusive relationship. P stated that she felt as if she had wasted her life, and she never envisioned her marriage ending in divorce.

Mourning the loss of their partners, their dreams, and their realities is not pathological for battered woman but a natural progression in the process of change. Women need optimum support at this stage. With or without support, some battered women may consider going back to their abusive partners and others might return for "one more try." Moreover, women might remain physically attracted to their partners and renew sexual involvement with them.

The action stage is the busiest and least stable of the stages. It carries the highest risk for relapse. Helping relationships continue, but practitioners introduce the behavioral interventions called counter-conditioning and stimulus control for the first time in the change process (Connors et al., 2001). Clients need to depend on helping relationships more than ever (Prochaska et al., 2002). According to Goodman and Fallon (1995), assertiveness training, group support, and grieving losses with others are helpful interventions at this stage of the change process.

Maintenance

In this stage, battered women assume responsibility for their lives and begin moving forward. They present as changed people, envisioning a future without physical violence and psychological denigration. For example,

> R had endured a long, violent, and denigrating relationship with her ex-boyfriend. She was finally able to leave the relationship, secure a job, and get an apartment for her and her two children. She stated she wanted to focus on her children. She vowed never to get into an abusive relationship again. R stated, "I've learned the warning signs."

Clients also rely on new skills while attempting to prevent relapse. Self-reevaluation is a useful tool here because clients are constructing new identities and visions for their lives. In this stage, the helping relationship helps prevent relapse (Prochaska et al., 2002). The focus has shifted to a broader spectrum of problems beyond those related to their abusive partners. The maintenance stage is the opportune time to work on the multiple problems that contributed to or resulted from years of abuse. Resolving long-standing beliefs that undermined self-esteem and confidence, coping with fears and anxieties, addressing possible post-traumatic stress disorders, dealing with familial problems, and understanding the aftermath of abusive relationships are important targets of long-term treatment.

Future planning focuses on self-sufficiency, skill enhancement, strength building, career planning, and assertiveness training. Here, practitioners introduce strategies for obtaining housing, job training, and additional education. Feminist counseling and family therapy work if reunification is the family's goal, but only if all members participate in treatment and practitioners have equalized the woman's power base. If all members of the family are empowered, men can find healthier ways to deal with emotions, and women can continue to demonstrate their resolve not to live with violence (Smith, Williams & Rosen, 1990).

Termination

If clients have revised their attitudes and self-images, they are likely ready to terminate. Clients are no longer tempted to return to old behaviors or old feelings such as sadness, anger, or anxiety. A new lifestyle is essential for termination, and clients demonstrate genuine confidence in themselves (Prochaska et al., 2002). For battered women, this includes forgiveness.

After years of being hypervigilant, careful of every word spoken, and protecting their partners from painful situations and feelings, battered women often feel a range of emotions from relief to grace and gratitude. They also view their partners differently. Their partner's three faces fuse into one. Clients realize that these faces are facets of the same person. They can see their partners' strengths and forgive their deficits.

In reality, most battered women do not fully forgive their partners. However, forgiveness is an essential part of the healing process (Witvliet, Ludwig & Vander Laan, 2001; Coates, 1997). According to Dutton (1995), whether battered women ends violence by staying with their partners or leaving, they demonstrate their changes through resolve, directness, and balance. These women have no fear of their partners, having moved past their hatred. A spiritual connectedness emerges, with an appropriate assignment of responsibility. Formerly battered women can name their role in the violence and forgive their partners.

With termination and forgiveness, they hold their partners accountable for their violence. However, at the same time, formerly battered women understand that their abusive partners also frequently felt completely powerless. Dutton (1995) stated that as battered women move through the stages of change and find themselves beyond their abuse, they resemble people who have completed twelve-step programs. That is, battered women find peace and serenity.

Questions

The authors just presented their version of the transtheoretical model related to treating domestic violence. In addition to the authors' interpretation of this model, find and read the original authors' ideas about this model. Complete a summary of the stages of change model taken directly from the literature.

1. Compare the original with the authors' interpretation. What differences, if any, did you find and what are they? Did the authors leave anything out or misinterpret the model in any way? If so, what did they forget or misinterpret?

2. What is your professional opinion of this model as it pertains to working with domestic violence? Discuss your ideas with classmates in the full class or small groups.

3. According to the professional literature, what other approaches does the literature recommend for work with battered women? Compare the tenets and beliefs of these models with the transtheoretical model explicated here. What are the major similarities and differences between the models and approaches to treatment?

Engaging Mikki in Treatment

The morning after her arrival, I interviewed Mikki in my office. My office was our primary meeting place for the next year and a half. Mikki still appeared scared and nervous. I pointed her to a couch in my office and sat down next to her. I tried to put her at ease by engaging her in small talk. I explained to her my role and function at the shelter, the rules of the shelter, and the services we offered. This gave Mikki what Schulman (1992) called "handles for work." By explaining the purpose and function of the practitioner and agency, clients may find something helpful in the explanation that they can use. In retrospect, I provided Mikki information and should have given her more opportunity to ask questions. Allowing clients to ask questions helps test their level of understanding, clear up misunderstandings, and begin learning about their goals.

Mikki's Personal History

During our interview, I learned more about Mikki's background. She spoke slowly and haltingly, often having problems finding the right words. Gradually, her history emerged.

Mikki complained about lifelong weight problems. She could not remember a time when she was not on some type of diet. Her weight was a source of ridicule and taunting by classmates throughout school.

Mikki did not talk much about her father. He died when she was thirteen and was never around much before his death. Nikki said that she and her mother frequently argued, but to her knowledge, there was no physical violence in her parent's relationship. She recalled that her father's drinking was a problem and caused many family arguments.

Mikki believed that her mother "never really liked her" and was ashamed of her because of her weight. Her mother frequently compared Mikki to her brother who, according to Mikki, was the "perfect child." Her brother, who was three years older, attended college but did not graduate. However, he secured a job in banking and was apparently doing well. He was married with two children. Mikki seldom saw or talked with him, only on holidays at her mother's house.

Beginnings of Physical Abuse

Mikki got married when she was 24 years old. She met her future husband at a church social event. They married six months later. According to Mikki, her mother did not approve of the marriage because of "ethnic differences." Mikki's family was German descent and her husband was Polish. According to Mikki, her in-laws had the same concerns. Her husband's extended family constantly reminded her of their familial differences, made jokes about her weight, and implied that their son did her a favor by marrying her.

About six months into the marriage, Mikki's husband became more "controlling." He forbade Mikki from speaking to her friends. He particularly disliked the woman Mikki lived with before her current hospitalization. The physical violence started innocently. He began "pushing and shoving" her during arguments. This escalated to slaps in the face, often leaving Mikki with black eyes. This progressed to "full out" beatings by the time she decided to leave the marriage. The physical violence was accompanied by psychological violence in the form of name calling and "put downs" in front of his family and friends. Her husband's family knew about the violence but neither said nor did anything to stop it. Mikki once told her mother about the violence. Her mother responded by saying, "Well, you married him."

Mikki decided to leave when her husband beat her up, kicked her in the sides and stomach, and locked her in a closet for two hours. The following morning when her husband left for work, Mikki called her friend for a place to live, packed a few belongings, and left. Her friend had told her about a surgery for people with severe weight problems and helped her find a job at a neighborhood resale shop. When her husband discovered that she was having surgery, he tried to have her removed from his insurance plan. However, since they were still married, he could do nothing to stop her. After surgery, Mikki had to quit her job because she could not stand for protracted lengths of time.

Physical Abuse Escalated

Just before surgery, Mikki met and began dating Don. Her friend did not like him because he was African American. She did not want Don in her house, claiming that it was not safe for him to come into her neighborhood. Mikki commented, "I think she was more concerned about what the neighbors would say than about what would happen to Don." While she was recovering from surgery in the hospital, Mikki's friend called to tell her that she needed to find somewhere else to live. Mikki received this call two days before discharge, but was afraid and ashamed to tell the hospital staff that she was virtually homeless.

Mikki said that Don also became physically and psychologically abusive. When pressed for details of the abuse, she was reticent. She did claim that Don was better, "at least, he didn't hit me in the face." She talked at length about his sense of humor, love of her cooking, and how much he taught her about the city. She wanted to know if the shelter provided counseling for men, stating, "He just gets a little upset at times, but he always apologizes. My husband never apologized." Mikki never called the police about the abuse she suffered from either her husband or boyfriend.

Questions

Now that the authors have presented more information about Mikki, perform the following exercises based on your education, experience, the profes-

sional literature, and the available best practices evidence. To increase your learning potential, you may want to do this in a small group with other students.

1. Based on the information contained above, construct a three-generation genogram and eco-map that represent Mikki's personal, familial, and environmental circumstances. What further information do you need to complete this exercise? What patterns do these two important graphical assessment tools demonstrate?

2. Building on your earlier work, complete a list of Mikki's issues and strengths, drawing from multi-systemic sources.

3. Write a two- to three-page narrative assessment that encompasses Mikki's multi-systemic issues and strengths. Review Chapter 1 if needed. This narrative should provide a comprehensive and multi-systemic explanation of her life as she prepares to undergo therapy with the authors.

4. Based on your assessment, construct an initial treatment plan for Mikki.

Initial Treatment Planning

I remember listening to Mikki's narrative and wondering how she could praise this man since he was probably beating her on a regular basis. I advised Mikki that abuse only becomes worse. What began as a push often ends in serious injury or death. I also reminded her of the pattern of abuse started by her husband. I reiterated the services of the shelter and pointed out services that I felt would be beneficial to her. We established a verbal contract with the following goals:

1. The shelter would provide her a temporary safe environment. In return, Mikki had to abide by shelter rules (e.g., doing chores around the shelter, adhering to curfew hours; not initiating contact with the abusive partner).
2. Mikki would obtain employment training.
3. Mikki would obtain housing.
4. Mikki would keep medical appointments.
5. Mikki would attend a support group at the shelter.

I believed that these goals would ultimately be important to help Mikki reach independence from her abusive partner. I based this work on research that found that economic dependence played a major role for women remaining in abusive relationships (Barnett, 2000; Baker, 1997; Hadley et al., 1995). At that time, we also assumed that the best plan for a battered woman was to leave her partner and stay away from him.

Questions

Earlier in this chapter, the authors explicated a theory and practice model for working with battered women. Review their model and apply it to the following exercise.

1. Based on their model, what mistakes (in thinking and technique) were made during the first interview?

2. If you were the practitioner working with Mikki, how would you have approached this session? Explore and explain any differences between your approach and the authors.

3. What clues did Mikki offer the practitioner about her worldview, self-identity, self-image, and self-efficacy? Based on these clues, develop a different initial treatment plan that better fits her worldview.

4. Based on the author's model, at this point, what is your hunch about Mikki's stage of change? Please explain and defend your answer with specific examples taken from the first session.

Where Did I Go Wrong?

I made several mistakes in our initial interview that would become more glaring as my work proceeded with Mikki. When Mikki entered my life, I had been out of graduate school for four years and had worked at the shelter for six months. My previous work experience was in a family service agency. Since I received my graduate education at one of the top three schools of social work in the country, it provided the implicit message that my training and degree gave me a special knowledge to know what was best for clients. Ergo, I learned practitioner arrogance.

The Mistakes of Arrogance

According to Baker (1997), battered women live with a cultural script that dictates how they are "supposed" to extricate themselves from abusive relationships. That script was evident in the contract I devised for Mikki. That is, stay away from your partner, obtain a job, and secure housing. Believing this was the best course of action for her, I paid little, if any attention, to how Mikki defined her reality. I had no idea what Mikki wanted for herself.

In retrospect, Mikki provided clues about her reality throughout the course of our interview. There was a fissure in her view of Don. She focused on his good points (i.e., his sense of humor, his praise of her cooking, etc.), and discounted his abusive behavior, stating, "He gets a little upset at times." Based on her interest in counseling for men, I should have realized that she wanted to end the violence but not the relationship. Moreover, I do not believe that Mikki viewed herself as a battered woman.

I believe that Mikki was in the precontemplation stage of change (Prochaska et al., 2002). She was in denial, as demonstrated by her rationalizing and discounting the severity of her abuse in an effort to believe the good side of her abusive partner (Eisikovits & Buchbinder, 1999). Mikki felt the abuse from her boyfriend was better than the abuse by her husband because the boyfriend did not hit her in the face.

Additionally, I asked her to do things that were not ego-syntonic. She had never lived alone or had substantial employment. Suddenly, I embodied the dominant script by requiring her to do these things, whether she liked it or not. In addition, I should have considered her medical condition when I asked her to find full-time employment.

Mikki had struggled with severe weight problems all of her life. Rejection was an expectation rather than an exception. I needed to watch possible transference problems related to other authority figures in her life. Mikki had probably learned that any type of overt dissent meant rejection. I mainly saw her deficits, not her strengths, and decided that her support system was inadequate. In retrospect, I should have asked her what support, other than housing, her friend could provide and if she wanted to contact her friend. This would have given Mikki a voice in shaping her goals and objectives. By not considering Mikki's construct of reality and stage of change, I had devised a corrupt contact with Mikki (Compton & Galaway, 1989). While Mikki did not say that our contract differed from her agenda, her later actions spoke loud and clear.

The watchword of shelter work is empowerment. However, my work with Mikki was disempowering, replicating the abusive relationship with her boyfriend and husband. First, there was a power inequity between us. Mikki was vulnerable; she had medical challenges, no place to live, and her support network was limited. With the confluence of those factors, it was unlikely that she would overtly challenge the contract. To challenge the contract meant that she would be in the streets.

Shelter workers often find themselves in a paradoxical box. They want to facilitate empowerment but, at the same time, must devise goals and objectives that are in concert with the facility's policies and procedures. There is no easy way out of this box. However, practitioners must be cognizant that goals and objectives will have to be modified based on a client's stage of change. Knowing this would have attenuated much of the anger and frustration I felt toward Mikki.

Second, I discounted her feelings about Don. Don was an important part of Mikki's life and defined reality. Men who batter often discount their partners' feelings by saying the women are "crazy" or "stupid" for feeling a certain way or expressing an opinion. Often, abusive men do not consider the women's feelings (Black, 2001; Chang, 1996). Those tactics often lower self-esteem and confidence. While I did not describe Mikki as "stupid" or "crazy," my behavior conveyed my negative attitude about her life, behaviors, and attitudes. I did not encourage her to talk about Don's good side; I admonished her by talking about the escalation of violence. Hence, I failed to show compassion. Similar to many people in abusive relationships, Mikki returned to see me because she had no place else to go. In a sense, my arrogance placed me in the role of abuser.

The best approach for Mikki would have been to devise a safety plan and encourage her to tell her narrative (DiClemente & Velasquez 1991). Safety planning at this stage of change is important because women often return to their abusive partners. Allowing a client to relate her narrative gives a message that their life journey has worth and it validates their construct of reality. Hearing the narrative gives practitioners an idea of what is important to a client. The narrative begins the process of helping clients look at their life and their potential barriers toward change. I also could have provided Mikki with information about the dynamics of nonviolent relationships, that is, helping her discover ways that couples settle conflict without resorting to physical violence. This would have presented Nikki with a different definition of reality.

Further Contacts and Frustrations

I began working on my part of our contract: setting up an appointment with a job coach, exploring possible housing resources, and contacting the hospital social worker about clinic appointments. Mikki attended one group session. However, the following week she claimed that she did not feel well and did not come downstairs for the meeting. Staff believed she was feigning illness. The group facilitator said that Mikki had not said much in the group the week before. However, when she did speak, Mikki minimized the abuse and defended her boyfriend. This behavior is common for battered women in the precontemplation stage of change (Ryan et al., 1995; Simpson & Joe, 1993; Johnson, 1986).

As stated previously, it was too early in Mikki's change process for group therapy. She wanted affirmation that abuse was not happening and assurance that she could save her relationship. Those who work with battered women must understand that change entails shedding the old self and trying on the new self (Connors et al., 2001). In essence, we ask clients to reconstruct their identity and lives.

Mikki diligently kept her medical clinic appointments. She did well in outpatient physical therapy; continued to be independent; and did more stair climbing than earlier. However, her side effects from surgery (nausea, diarrhea, and emesis) continued. In addition, doctors diagnosed her with idiopathic scoliosis, an abnormal curvature of the spine, which caused her to walk with a slight listing to the right. Doctors also diagnosed Mikki with carpal tunnel syndrome, a condition that causes pain, numbness, and weakness in the fingers or hands and occasionally in the forearm and elbow.

After returning from a visit with her physician, Mikki reported that the physician felt she was unable to work and suggested that she explore Supplemental Security Insurance (SSI). According to Mikki, her physician believed that her scoliosis and surgery precluded long periods of standing. In addition, the carpal tunnel syndrome would exacerbate if she had to do repetitive hand and finger movements. The physician was also concerned about the continued side effects of her surgery. He told Mikki that he might have to consider reversing the surgery if they persisted. Therefore, the goal of obtaining employment was replaced with the goal of obtaining disability.

In the following weeks, I worked with Mikki and the hospital social worker on procuring the necessary documents for disability benefits (e.g., medical reports, birth certificates, marriage certificate). I also referred her to an agency that provided housing for low-income and disabled individuals.

Mikki Disappears

On the day of Mikki's appointment to apply for disability, I provided carfare for the appointment and lunch money. By 6:00 p.m., she had not returned to the shelter. When she had not returned by 8:00 p.m., we began to worry. We discussed calling the police and reporting her as a missing person. Ultimately, we decided that Mikki was a competent adult who had not been missing for twenty-four hours. If she did not show up or contact the shelter the next day, we could call the police.

Around 10:00 p.m. that evening, Mikki called the shelter and asked to speak to me. Mikki decided to return to her boyfriend. They had talked and he promised to do better. Mikki asked again about counseling services for men. I could feel the anger rising in me from the pit of my stomach to my hairline. I had to control the tenor of my voice. I reminded her that the focus of the agency was to provide services for women. I reiterated the hackneyed admonishment about the escalation of violence, both in frequency and severity. Mikki simply replied, "I'll be okay . . . He's really trying to change." I attempted to get a telephone number from her, but she was calling from a pay phone and Don did not have a telephone. I remember hanging up the phone, just staring at it for several minutes, and thinking, "She's probably been in contact with him all along."

My Reaction

Soon, guilt and relief replaced my anger. I felt guilty because I believed that I had failed to help her. In retrospect, I also felt rejected by Mikki. I had spent an inordinate amount of time and effort in trying to procure services that, at least in my opinion, would help Mikki escape from domestic violence and facilitate her independence. I interpreted returning to the boyfriend as saying, "Your help was no good." Mikki had been a "difficult client" who had not followed the dominant cultural script (Baker, 1997). Now that she was out of the shelter, I felt relief in no longer having responsibility for her.

Questions

Obviously, Mikki did not engage in treatment at the shelter. Before reading on, answer the following questions.

1. Based on the case material, what hunches do you have about the reasons Mikki left the shelter? What could the practitioner have done differently to intervene in a positive way in this case?

2. What does the practice literature, in addition to the model provided here, have to say about engaging clients similar to Mikki in treatment?

3. Now that she returned home to an abusive partnership, what recourse do you have as the practitioner? Is there anything you should do for Mikki at this stage?

4. Search your beliefs and attitudes about domestic violence and battered women. In the context of you life and beliefs, respond to the author's honest account of her emotions after Mikki left treatment.

Safety Plan

The best intervention would have been to devise a safety plan. The plan would have included a "survival kit." A survival kit is a bag that battered women pack in anticipation of having to flee their home. The kit can contain clothing, toiletries, money, if available, and important documents, such as birth certificates, marriage certificate, social security cards, etc. Women hide the bag in a safe but accessible place in case they must leave home hurriedly. If available, they can leave their bag with a neighbor or a friend.

Safety planning also entails assessing the structure and physical layout of the house or apartment and premapping escape routes. If neighbors are available or willing, a prearranged signal can be devised, such as flicking the lights on and off in a room. Screaming fire is another tactic. Neighbors and strangers are more likely to respond to "fire" than "help." However, many battered women are reluctant to use this tactic because of the shame associated with being beaten (Barnett, 2001; Baker, 1997). Nonetheless, loud and persistent screaming might spur otherwise disengaged neighbors to call the police. Today, dependent upon funding, many battered women's programs issue women cell phones that only dial 911.

If I had considered Mikki's stage of change, I should have expected her to return to Don. By not considering that factor, I was left feeling angry and frustrated with her and myself (Baker, 1997). Over the years, I have learned that practitioners must provide help, within legal and ethical perimeters, as defined by the client. Mikki did not want the help I offered. She wanted counseling for her boyfriend, but I refused to hear that plea.

Cue the "White Knight"

I had no contact with Mikki for several months. However, I frequently wondered how she was faring and if Don was beating her. On a cold February morning, a staff member rang my phone. Mikki was in the lounge and wanted to see me. I went to the lounge and found her sitting in a chair looking downcast and disheveled. When she stood up to go into my office, it was apparent that she had gained considerable weight. When we were in the office and seated, I began the interview by asking what had been happening in her life. Mikki gave the following narrative:

Since leaving the shelter eight months earlier, Mikki had lived with Don. According to Mikki, things went well for a while. Then, the psychological abuse began again. Don called her a "bitch," "fat," and "ugly." Soon, the physical abuse began again.

Mikki had been awarded SSI disability. She got a lump-sum payment and was receiving a monthly check. She also received Medicaid. Mikki said that most of their arguments involved her monthly check. Mikki had the check, and Don wanted it. She estimated that Don slapped or punched her at least two times a week.

Since her side effects did not abate, she also had surgery to reverse her intestinal bypass. Since having the reversal surgery, she had regained most of the weight she lost. Mikki said, "I know I look awful. Maybe, if I lost some weight, Don wouldn't be so short-tempered with me. Sometimes, I just don't have the energy to try to exercise and eating diet foods is expensive. I don't get too much with food stamps."

Two nights earlier, Don came home drunk. She voiced concern about the amount of money he spent on alcohol when there were unpaid bills. Don punched her in the stomach, causing her to fall over a table. When she was on the floor, he began kicking her. Mikki said, "I thought he was going to kill me this time. Maybe, I should have just kept my mouth shut."

When Don fell asleep, she slipped out of the apartment and walked to the emergency room of a hospital in the neighborhood. She told the triage nurse that she fell down the stairs. Her injuries were not serious enough to warrant admission to the hospital. Mikki spent the night in the hospital cafeteria. The next morning, she went to one of the warming centers run by the city. These shelters provided a place in the winter for homeless individuals. The centers provide meals and a place to sit. She ended up spending the night at a homeless shelter. When she left the shelter, Mikki went to a public library and then took the bus to the shelter. Mikki stated, "That shelter is scary. It has an ilk [sic] of people I don't wanna be around. A fight broke out and your stuff gets stole [sic] if you turn your back. Can I come back here?"

Our shelter was full. In addition, after she had left, shelter administrators decided not to readmit her. They believed that her medical challenges made Mikki better suited for an intermediate-level nursing home facility or a custodial residential facility. This was déjà vu. Again, Mikki sat before me dejected and homeless. Since she was not a resident of the shelter, I would have been within legal and ethical boundaries to provide carfare and refer her to a city agency that handled emergency shelter placements.

I was torn between concern for Mikki and my responsibility to the residents of the shelter. I was aware that working with her would consume an excessive amount of time and energy. I was not aware that I had an unconscious need to rescue her. In the end, concern won, and I mounted the "white horse." I asked Mikki what she wanted to do. She replied, "I need somewhere to go. I don't think I can go back with Don."

Initial Treatment Planning—Again

This time, I asked Mikki about her most pressing problem. She stated that she needed a place to stay. I wanted Mikki to name her problem. Clients often have more investment in treatment if they work on problems that they identify (Tolson, Reid &

Garvin, 2003). I also wanted to establish common ground with her. That is, Mikki and I agreed upon the problem. I hoped that our agreement would avoid another corrupt contract. I contacted a city agency that provided a broad range of emergency services, including housing.

The agency arranged a placement in a shelter for women and worked on finding Mikki space in a SRO (single room occupancy) hotel. At the time, SROs were prevalent in the city. These were hotels, often located in economically depressed areas of the city, that provided inexpensive rooms. Usually, there were no cooking facilities and bathrooms were shared. As regentrification occurred in the city, these hotels have virtually disappeared.

I asked Mikki if she would be interested in rejoining the battered women's group at the shelter. Mikki stated, "I really didn't care too much for that group. I don't do too good in groups. I'd rather just see you." Since she did not want to be in the group, I did not push her. We also talked about procuring housing that is more permanent. Her previous application for permanent housing had been approved, but since she could not be contacted, the application had been cancelled. Mikki agreed to the services offered by the city agency and stated she would reapply for permanent housing.

At that point, Mikki entered the contemplation stage of the change process. She was becoming aware that a problem existed but was feeling guilty and blaming herself for the violence (Prochaska et al., 2002). Her statements about her weight and keeping her mouth shut evinced that guilt and self-blaming. Mikki still viewed the violence as a separate entity from her boyfriend and took responsibility for his violence. If she could control her words ("Maybe, I should have just kept my mouth shut."), she could control Don's violence (Eisikovits & Buchbinder, 1999).

A support group would have been an appropriate intervention at that stage of Mikki's change process. The group could help her to identify her strengths and survival skills. Most important, it would have provided a place of membership in which she could have developed helping relationships with other women (Ucko, 1991). However, the group process would have forced her to begin to examine her situation. Mikki was not ready to take that step.

Locating housing is an intervention that would usually come at a later stage of the change process (i.e., action or maintenance stage). However, circumstances can catapult clients into activities associated with later stages of change (Prochaska et al., 2002). Mikki had a pressing need for housing, and that need demanded that she take steps. Those who work with battered women must understand that the stages of change are not discrete and successive. Clients move back and forth between stages, skip stages, or remain stuck in a particular stage.

Mikki Reappears—Again

Again, several months passed without having contact with Mikki. Then, one sunny June afternoon, a co-worker told me that Mikki was in the lounge and had asked to see me. I knew she had returned to her boyfriend and that she was probably homeless again. I could feel the anger in me rising, but I had learned from experience with Mikki that berating her and using scare tactics did not work. When we got into my office, Mikki said that she had stayed at the SRO for about a month. Many of the residents there were older, and some had drinking problems.

She said she was lonely and missed her boyfriend. She had been back with him for about three months. Mikki said that Don promised to get counseling but never followed through on the promise. The previous evening, they got into an argument. He threw a plate of food in her face and hit her on the side of her head with a pot. He also pushed her against the wall and began to strangle her. Neighbors heard the commotion and called the police.

When the police arrived, Mikki denied that she had been physically assaulted. She told the police that she and Don had been arguing and apologized for the noise. The police reprimanded both of them for disturbing the peace and left. That behavior was characteristic of the contemplation stage of change. Mikki said that Don did not assault her again that night.

When he left for work in the morning, Mikki took a bus to a shelter located in another area of the city. She had not taken any clothing or personal belongings and would only be allowed to stay at the shelter for a month. Mikki stated she had gotten a letter from the agency that provided permanent housing. She had an appointment but did not remember the date and had left the letter in the apartment. The manner in which Mikki had to leave her home on two occasions demonstrates the need to educate battered women on a safety plan and a survival kit. Mikki commented, "He didn't bother me last night, after the police left. I think they [police] scared him, but I'm scared to go back over there and try and get my stuff."

I asked Mikki her reason for not telling the police about the assault. I did not want to imply blame, but I needed to understand her reasoning. She stated, "I didn't want him to get in trouble. If he went to jail, he might lose his job, and that would make things worse. I love him, but I thought he was trying to kill me last night. I don't know if I can live with his [sic] jumping on me." Mikki's statement indicated a beginning recognition that the violence (i.e., "his jumping on me") belonged to her boyfriend and was not a separate entity from him (Eisikovits & Buchbinder, 1999). Mikki was beginning to recognize a problem, but her attachment to Don still existed.

At the time, I viewed the attachment as deviant and did not encourage her to talk about it. If I had acknowledged her feelings and encouraged her to talk about them, Mikki and I could have engaged in a dialogue about the pros and cons of her choices. This could have helped her to recognize the dissonance between what she wanted and what she had done. It also could have helped her to begin to envision a life without physical violence. I asked Mikki what she wanted to do. She replied, "I guess I'm going to need a place to stay, again."

I spent the remainder of the afternoon on the telephone with various agencies. The city agency refused to assist her, having deemed her behavior as "frivolous and flighty." The police escorted Mikki to her apartment so that she could get her belongings and vital papers.

Over the next couple of weeks, Mikki came to the shelter and asked to see me. During that time, she had a limited range of affect; the cadence of her speech was slower; and she seemed to have more problems than usual finding words. She complained of not sleeping well and feeling "down." She had an appointment with the housing agency in about two weeks and expressed anxiety about the interview and the type of questions they would ask her. She feared that they would reject her because her clothing was not appropriate for the interview.

If I could not see her immediately, Mikki would wait until I was free. This meant that I stayed late at work many nights. This happened two or three times per week. Again, I was becoming frustrated and angry with Mikki. Her behavior was draining my physical and psychological energy. I felt as if I was the only person in her support network. I needed to confront her but did not know how because I was afraid she might be suicidal. I had become Mikki's "white knight," and she relied on me to save her from her abusive relationship.

Questions

The author became Mikki's "White Knight", riding up on her steed to save the day and make Mikki over in the image portrayed by the dominant script the author mentioned earlier. Almost everyone who enters the helping professions begins their careers carrying an emotional and spiritual "Save the World Card." Similar to being someone's white knight, your "Save the World Card" entitles you to believe that you are the only person in the world able to help your clients.

Furthermore, your "Save the World" club membership entitles you to believe that you can help everyone to a better life, as defined by you or the practice texts. Fortunately, most people that last in the helping professions ultimately resign from the club and burn their "Save the World Card." Assume you were the practitioner working with Mikki, complete with your royal steed, and "Save the World Card" in tow.

1. What steps would you take at this moment to improve your work with Mikki? Be specific and discuss your reasons for each step.

2. If you have given up your "Save the World Card" or sold your body armor, what made you take this step? Describe the client or circumstance that forced you to understand the limits of your power over people and how you handled this situation. Engage classmates in small-group discussions about their experiences, similar or different.

Consultation and Self-Examination

The shelter utilized a consultant for so-called difficult cases. I believed that Mikki met the criteria. After obtaining permission from the shelter director, I met the consultant. I verbalized my concerns about Mikki's dependency on me and my fears that she might be suicidal. The consultant asked if the client hinted or spoke about suicide, either threats or ideas. Mikki had talked about feeling "down" and that her weight caused Don to abuse her. However, she did not have high risk factors in her history, including a history of suicide attempts, psychiatric hospitalizations, history of substance abuse, family history of suicide, and/or verbalization of a suicide plan or fantasies about death (Bongar, 1991).

The consultant inquired if I had asked her about suicide. When I replied that I had not, she talked about the fear of opening "Pandora's box" and letting out the "fates." Often, practitioners avoid asking clients questions because they fear the answers and dread feeling responsible for "fixing" the client's problems. She suggested that I examine my need to rescue this client, pointing out that Mikki's life belonged to Mikki. She pointed out other areas for self-examination, including my values and my own experience with interpersonal violence. Was female independence (e.g., education and employment) important to me? The consultant posed a very poignant question, "Because of your values, are you trying to turn this woman into a clone of yourself?"

I told the consultant that I felt as if I was Mikki's only support system, and if I confronted her, she might sink into a deeper depression, possibly leading to suicide. In essence, the consultant told me that I was flattering myself too much. She believed that Mikki had a dependent personality and if I were not around, Mikki would find someone else to attach to.

The consultant encouraged me to set boundaries in terms of when I would see her, what tasks I would perform, and what tasks she would perform. She felt that Mikki would adhere to boundaries because people with a dependent personality often have a desire to please those in authority and seldom overtly demonstrate defiance (Morrison, 1995). The consultant did not feel that Mikki was a high risk for suicide but agreed to see her if there were marked changes in her affect, behavior, or verbalization.

The consultant pointed out that Mikki was facing very difficult situations but did possess strengths. Mikki had survived 30 years of life. She survived intermittent periods of homelessness. In fact, she had arranged her own placement in the shelter. With direction and encouragement, Mikki could follow through with obtaining SSI and making an application for housing. The consultant suggested that I look at ways to use her strengths to enhance her decision-making and planning skills.

Finally, the consultant addressed the difficult and sensitive subject of race. She pointed out that ethnic identity was a salient factor in Mikki's life. Part of the conflict in her marriage was because she married someone from a different ethnicity. Mikki lived in a city that had many ethnic groups and races, but the city was far from a multi-cultural nirvana. That is, the various racial and ethnic groups kept to themselves and seldom interacted with those outside their group. Moreover, there was often conflict between racial and ethnic groups.

The consultant posed the question of how Mikki's ethnic identity might influence how she viewed the world and her decision-making. In other words, given

Mikki's background, what was the significance of her having a boyfriend from a different race or ethnicity?

The consultant also pointed out that I needed to assess my own feelings about interracial dating and marriage. I also needed to think about how Mikki might view me as a professional woman-of-color. Mikki had never given any indication that she had problems having a practitioner-of-color. However, I had encountered Caucasian clients who engaged in a type of stereotype substitution. From their conversation and behavior, they expected a certain degree of "magic" from me. In many ways, this was a "left-handed compliment" because the subtext of the compliment contained the stereotype that people-of-color do not excel. If one does excel, (s)he must be endowed with exceptional powers and abilities (Moore, 1998).

The meeting with the consultant raised many questions about the client and myself that I had not consciously considered. Those issues would be germane in work with future clients. I had to admit to myself that I did have a hidden agenda for Mikki. I wanted her to be independent and self-sufficient. That agenda was not Mikki's agenda at that point in her life. I began to understand that Mikki had ownership of her life. She had the right of choice, and when the result of her choices might be less than desired, my role as a social worker was to help her consider alternatives. I think I began that day to glean the meaning of positive regard.

Termination/Outcome/Follow-Up

In my next meeting with Mikki, I attempted to implement some of the consultant's suggestions. I began with setting boundaries. I acknowledged Mikki's difficult situation but pointed out that I also had responsibilities for the women at the shelter. I was willing to continue to work with her, but we would have to set a structure for our meetings. We would set appointments for her to see me at the shelter. If she was unable to keep an appointment, she should call me. If she needed to talk with me between appointments, she would telephone me, and if I was unavailable, she should leave a number where I could call her back. Residents at the shelter where Mikki lived had access to telephones to make calls related to employment, counseling, etc.

For several years, Mikki's life had been chaotic. She had crises in her life, but she perceived almost every problem as a crisis. Living in domestic violence is to live in chaos. Long-term abuse can result in deficits in decision-making. Problems that others could negotiate become major obstacles for the battered woman (Koss et al., 1994).

By seeing her when she came to the shelter unannounced, I reinforced her chaos and her perception of crises. By bringing structure to our relationship, I modeled how Mikki could bring some structure to her life. By having scheduled times to meet, we could collaborate on strategies, weigh the pros and cons, and try to execute those strategies in a less frenetic manner. As the consultant predicted, Mikki did not verbally challenge the boundaries I set.

Next, I addressed my concern about Mikki possibly trying to harm herself. I told her that I noticed how sad she appeared. Then, I opened "Pandora's box" by asking the question, "Have you thought about hurting yourself?" Mikki looked at me for a moment and replied, "You mean, kill myself? I've been feeling pretty down, but no. I couldn't do that. I'm Catholic. There's a church near the shelter, and sometimes, I go in there to pray." I asked her what she prayed for. Mikki said she prayed that she would feel better physically, that Don would stop fighting her, and for a place to live. Mikki's faith was another strength. I had not considered Mikki's religious beliefs as a potential resource for her.

She was a member of a religion with a strong taboo against suicide. The taboo was not an absolute guarantee that she would not harm herself, but it might motivate her to seek other ways to address her problems. In addition, Mikki's religion might provide a social network. However, her prayers also indicated that she was still hoping for a life with her boyfriend. At that point, Mikki was probably vacillating between the contemplation and preparation stages of the change process.

We also discussed safety planning. I commended her on her ability to locate shelter herself. I pointed out how she had been able to address a difficult problem and find, at least, a temporary resolution. Clients are often more aware of their deficits than their strengths, and a major task of the social worker is to highlight a client's strengths (Saleebey, 1997). By pointing out Mikki's problem-solving skills in one situation, she might transfer those skills in addressing future problems.

We discussed the possibility that she might have future contact with her boyfriend and ways that she could try to get away from him if he became violent. I pointed out that her new apartment could become part of her safety plan. Mikki had a pattern of giving up her own housing and moving in with her boyfriend. If she did decide to have contact with her boyfriend, she might want to consider keeping her own apartment. Having her own apartment might prevent periods of homelessness for her.

I tried to facilitate her empowerment by encouraging her to devise her own solutions. However, for many clients "the problem" can become all-encompassing and a barrier to them in finding alternative solutions. One practitioner role is to offer possible alternative solutions. Practitioner suggestions can also help clients begin to consider an alternative reality (Gallant, 1993).

Her ability to execute that strategy at that stage of her change process was questionable. Men who batter often demand immediate gratification from their partners; thus, battered women learn to be present-focused and demonstrate difficulty with more long-range, future oriented planning (Connors et al., 2001). Nevertheless, the suggestion was something Mikki might consider at a later stage of her change process.

Other resources, such as an Order of Protection, hotline services, and groups for battered women, were discussed, and she was given a booklet on services for battered women. Mikki was probably not ready to use most of those resources. However, research has shown that often women feel more empowered by knowing what resources are available to them through the service delivery system (Black,

2001; Davies et al., 1998; Hadley et al., 1995). Ideally, this conversation should have occurred early in the intervention with this client. However, most of my past contacts with Mikki had been done in a frenetic atmosphere, and the focus had been on getting her shelter from the streets.

It should be noted that this appointment with Mikki and subsequent appointments and telephone conversations were more case management sessions than therapy sessions. Psychotherapy is an intervention of the preparation stage and can be effective when a woman is ready to evaluate underlying issues in her relationship with her abusive partner (Connors et al., 2001). At the time I worked with Mikki, she was not ready to examine how the confluence of family history, a lifelong struggle with weight, and ethnic/racial identity factored into her relationship with her current boyfriend.

The Changes

Mikki never appeared at my office again without an appointment. Between appointments, she contacted me frequently by telephone. She would give a detailed presentation of what she had done. I would praise her and point out the skills she had used to address whatever issue. In subsequent sessions, we addressed the interview for her apartment, completing necessary paper work, setting a medical appointment, and changing her mailing address for her SSI check.

A major concern for Mikki was the upcoming interview for the apartment. She was concerned about what to wear and what questions would be asked. Mikki and I did a simulation of the interview, and I used contingency planning, posing "what if" questions. I asked Mikki how she would handle various situations and would sometimes suggest alternatives. I used active listening, rephrasing what she had said, to make sure I understood her. I would ask her to feedback to me information that I had given her to ensure she understood me. Often I would ask Mikki to provide a rationale for tasks she had to perform and would explain how the tasks were related to her goals. Making her more aware of what steps she needed to take to address an issue was a method of enhancing her problem-solving skills (Tolson et al., 2003). According to Connors et al. (2001), a vital role of the helper in the preparation stage of change is to assess the client's ability to implement change strategies and to remedy skill deficits.

Living with domestic violence often means that women must deny their emotions while becoming alienated from their feelings (Connors et al., 2001). Mikki stated that she was concerned about what she would wear to the interview for the apartment; however, her underlying feeling was shame about the weight she had gained. We discussed her health concerns and the need to continue seeing her physician. I encouraged Mikki to make a list of her concerns and take the list with her when she saw her physician.

The shelter kept clothing for women, and Mikki was able to find something that she liked, which fit her well. She kept the appointment with the housing agency and was accepted as a resident. I referred her to various agencies that could help her with furniture and household items. Mikki did not have a telephone in her apartment, and when she called me, she had to use a public phone. The telephone calls became less frequent but still quite lengthy.

In one conversation, Mikki disclosed that she was seeing Don again, but that she was not living with him. She stated, "I never want to be on the streets again. It's so scary out there. You don't know where you're going to sleep or if you'll get hurt. You don't even know where you gonna [sic] use the bathroom." That statement provided me with a window into Mikki's reality and experience. I began to understand how frightened she must have been and the courage she needed to keep trying. Before our conversation ended, I reviewed her safety plan.

Termination

Mikki did not call for several weeks, and in the interim, I accepted a position at another agency. I was hoping that Mikki would call so that we could have closure. Mikki did call before I left the shelter. As with previous conversations, she provided minute details on her activities. She had reconnected with her friend with whom she had lived following her initial surgery. Mikki said she was still seeing her boyfriend. I did not ask her if he was still hurting her. I guess I was afraid of opening "Pandora's box" again. I told Mikki that I was leaving the shelter and reiterated some of the resources available for battered women. I asked if she had given any more thought to participating in a group for battered women. Mikki was silent for a moment and then said, "I'll think about it. Good luck to you." Over the years, I have thought about Mikki and wished her good luck.

Evaluation of Practice

I did not use measurement instruments (e.g., task attainment scaling, goal attainment scaling, depression scales) to track Mikki's progress through the treatment process. Progress was tracked by my observation of her behavior and tasks in which she was able to engage at a given time. At termination, Mikki was beginning to enter the preparation stage of change. However, she moved back and forth between stages of change, particularly between precontemplation and contemplation. Mikki performed some tasks that were characteristic of the action or maintenance stage of change (e.g., locating housing).

Though her situation forced her to perform that advanced task, she did not exhibit behaviors or execute other tasks associated with the later stages of change (e.g., an awareness of the danger of living in a violent intimate relationship, focus on the future, or a desire to explore underlying issues). According to Prochaska et al. (2002), in order to affect change, the helper must implement the right intervention at the right time. I question if Mikki would had advanced further and more quickly through the change process if I had implemented interventions that are more appropriate.

In addition, the structure of the service delivery system was an issue in working with this client. That structure does not easily accommodate the ambivalence of the change process. That structure is linear, having sequential steps to reach a goal, and does not tolerate vacillation. For example, the city agency that secured temporary housing for the client refused to help her once she went back to her boyfriend. The shelter where I worked did not have procedures in place to support workers who were simultaneously working with women in the shelter and those who were no longer residents.

Relevance of the Model: Implications for Practice with Battered Women

The stages of change encountered by battered women appear to parallel those identified by the authors of the transtheoretical change model. The model presented in this chapter relies on practice wisdom and observations from working with battered women in a shelter environment. We presented a framework for integrating constructivist theory and the transtheoretical change model in work with battered women. Since these clinical observations are not representative of all battered women, more studies should focus on how battered women navigate the change process.

Studies are needed to examine myriad populations of battered women (e.g., those who present to emergency rooms, trauma centers or physicians' offices; those who become involved in the legal justice system; those who make a decision to remain in their relationships). In addition, we must consider the influences of race, ethnicity, and age.

This model also has several implications for practitioners and agencies. The question often asked about a battered woman is, "Why does she stay?" Perhaps the new questions should be, "What does she want and need, and how does she cope and change over time?" To implement principles of constructivist theory and the transtheoretical change model, practitioners must examine their own values regarding violence, relationships, and personal choice. Working with battered women often challenges personal and professional values. Practitioners easily are caught between the ethical dilemma of respecting the client's right of self-determination and autonomy and the practitioner's responsibility to protect the client. Practitioners must somehow resolve those dilemmas if they are to engage in client-centered practice. To conduct client-centered practice is to make a conscious decision to give primacy to the client's wishes, within legal and ethical parameters.

In addition, practitioners must redefine "successful outcome." Defining success as the battered woman permanently leaving her abusive partner instead of, attaining a client-defined goal, narrowly defines successful outcome. The battered woman must have a voice in defining her success. Including the voice of the battered women exemplifies a collaborative relationship between the practitioner and client. If practitioners implement stage-specific interventions, they may have to expand their repertoire of interventions or form linkages with resources to provide those interventions. Forming more collaborative, client-centered relationships with battered women may help to prevent or lessen burnout in shelter workers and others who work with this population.

When battered women and practitioners have the same goals, there are no hidden agendas. Clients have a vital role in establishing and achieving their goals. By implementing stage-specific interventions, a practitioner will not be angry and disappointed with a woman in denial and that returns to her partner after one day in a shelter or a woman who displays anger toward her partner but resists change. Furthermore, practitioners will refocus from constructing the battered woman as totally helpless and inept to seeing her as an individual with strengths who is capable of making decisions and life changes with appropriate help.

Implementing principles from constructivist theory and the transtheoretical change model will also demand modifications in agency culture and policy. Agency administrators must make a critical assessment of policies that delimit women's choices. In today's practice world, brief treatment is often the mantra. Unfortunately, this is often based more on economics than clients' needs. Practitioners may need to be involved with battered women over a longer period, and agencies need to implement formal structures for client follow-up.

Battered women may need sequential brief treatment in which there are multiple encounters with a practitioner. This model could be more expensive to implement in the short-run because more choices and longer involvement with clients often mean higher operating costs. Agency administrators may have to do more education with funders in terms of helping them redefine successful outcomes and the importance of client-centered practice.

Moreover, agency administrators must be aware that implementing client-centered practice could have potential problems. Supporting a woman's choice to return to a violent relationship could make the agency and practitioners vulnerable for litigious activities from the families of battered women, battered women themselves, or their abusive partners. Therefore, administrators must take responsibility to ensure that their staffs understand the laws related to domestic violence. In addition, documentation, especially of safety planning, becomes paramount.

This model also has implication for social work education. Aphorisms in which social work students are frequently indoctrinated are "start where the client is," "respect the client," and "individualized treatment." Students must learn the specific skills and techniques needed to truly empathize with and respect clients. Research studies have shown that principles from constructivist theory and the transtheoretical change model have been effective in working with various client populations. By understanding how a client views their reality, students are in a better position to start where the client is. Moreover, by implementing collaborative strategies in concert with people's stage of change, students can demonstrate respect and individualized treatment planning in the context of client-centered services.

Questions

The author presented an interesting case involving domestic violence and the issues often associated with it in practice. Taking a broad view of this case, reevaluate the author's work and your participation, through the questions asked, throughout the case.

1. Take a moment to review Mikki's progress in treatment. Based on the author's description, the professional literature, and the latest practice evidence, what occurred to account for her progress?

2. What was the theoretical approach or combination of approaches that appeared to work best for Mikki?

3. Based on the work you have done earlier, what additional interventions would you recommend? Use the literature and latest evidence to justify your recommendations.

4. Overall, what is your professional opinion of the work performed in this case? As always, refer to the professional literature, practice evidence, your experience, and the experience of classmates when developing your opinion.

5. Based on this review, what additional or alternative approaches could have been used with this case? That is, if you were the practitioner, how would you have approached this case? Please explain and justify your approach.

6. What did this case demonstrate that you could use in other practice settings? List the most important things you learned by studying this case and how you could use them in your practice career.

Epilogue

I presented this case, highlighting many of my foibles, because students and experienced practitioners frequently make them in their work with battered women. Whether this case was "successful" is moot. The answer lies in how we define "success." If success is defined as Mikki never seeing her boyfriend again, obtaining additional education and employment, and living happily ever after, this case was stellar failure. If we define success in terms of what I learned from Mikki, the case was a stellar success.

Probably, Mikki helped me more than I helped her. She not only taught me things about her, but she also taught me things about myself. These gifts from Mikki were tools that I used in later work with battered women. She gave me the gift of understanding that change is often slow, painful, and scary for a battered woman. She also presented me with the gift of humility. Though I may have the education and training, ultimately, battered women are the experts on their life. If you are willing to learn, they will share their expertise, at no charge.

Bibliography

Baker, P. L. (1997). And I went back: Battered women's negotiation of choice. *Journal of Contemporary Ethnography, 26*(1), 55–74.

Barnett, O. W. (2000). Why battered women do not leave, Part 1: External inhibiting factors within society. *Trauma, Violence and Abuse, 1*(4), 343–372.

Barnett, O. W. (2001). Why battered women do not leave, Part 2: External inhibiting factors social support and internal inhibiting factors. *Trauma, Violence and Abuse, 2*(1), 3–35.

Bennett, L., Goodman, L., & Dutton, M. A. (1999). Systemic obstacles to the criminal prosecution of a battering partner: A victim perspective. *Journal of Interpersonal Violence, 14*(7), 761–772.

Bennett, L., & Lawson, M. (1994). Barriers to cooperation between domestic violence and substance abuse programs. *Families in Society: The Journal of Contemporary Human Services, 75*(5), 277–286.

Bongar, B. (1991). *The suicidal patient.* Washington, DC: American Psychological Association.

Black, C. J. (2001). The relationship between battered women and court advocates: What battered women find helpful. *Family Violence & Sexual Assault Bulletin, 17*(4), 8–16.

Brown, C., & O'Brien, K. M. (1998). Understanding stress and burnout in shelter workers. *Professional Psychology: Research & Practice, 29*(4), 383–385.

Brown, J. (1997). Working toward freedom from violence. *Violence Against Women, 3*(1), 5–26.

Browne, A. (1987). *When battered women kill.* New York: Free Press.

Browne, A., & Williams, K. (1989). Exploring the effects of resource availability and the likelihood of female-perpetrated homicides. *Law and Science Review, 23*(1), 75–94.

Burke, J. G., Gielen, A. C., McDonell, K. A., O'Campo, P., & Maman, S. (2001). The process of ending abuse in intimate relationships: A qualitative exploration of the Transtheoretical Model. *Violence Against Women, 7*(10), 1144–1163.

Busch, N. B. (2001). Battered women's moral reasoning: Conceptions and considerations of "right" and "wrong." *Dissertation Abstracts International, 62*(2-A), 772. (UMI No. 04194209)

Chang, V. N. (1996). *I just lost myself: Psychological abuse of women in marriage.* Westport, CT: Praeger Publishers.

Chornesky, A. (2000). The dynamics of battering revisited. *Affilia Journal of Women and Social Work, 15*(4), 480–501.

Coates, D. (1997). The correlations of forgiveness of self, forgiveness of others, and hostility, depression, anxiety, self-esteem, life adaptation, and religiosity among female victims of domestic violence. *Dissertation Abstracts International, 58*(5-B), 2667.

Compton, B. R., & Galaway, B. (1989). *Social work processes* (4th ed). Belmont, CA: Wadsworth.

Connors, G. J., Donovan, D. M., & DiClemente (2001). *Substance abuse, treatment, and the stages of change: Selecting and planning interventions.* New York: Guilford Press.

Davies, J., Lyon, E., & Monti, C. D. (1998). *Safety planning with battered women: complex lives/difficult choices.* Thousand Oaks, CA: Sage.

de Shazer, S. (1988). *Clues: Investigating solutions in brief therapy.* New York: W. W. Norton.

Dekel, R., & Peled, E. (2000). Staff burnout in Israeli battered women's shelter. *Journal of Social Service Research, 26*(3), 65–76.

DiClemente, C. C., & Prochaska, J. O. (1985). Processes and stages of change: Coping and competence in smoking behavior change. In S. Shiffman & T. A. Wills (Eds.), *Coping and substance abuse* (pp. 319–342). New York: Academic Press.

DiClemente, C. C., & Velasquez, M. M. (1991). Motivational interviewing and the stage of change. In W. R. Miller & S. Rollnick (Eds.), *Motivational interviewing: Preparing people to change addictive behavior* (pp. 201–216). New York: Guilford Press.

DiClemente, C. C., Story, M., & Murray, K. (2000). On a roll: The process of initiation and cessation of problem gambling among adolescents. *Journal of Gambling Studies, 16*(2/3), 289–313.

DiClemente, C. C., & Velasquez, M. M. (2002). Motivational interviewing and the stage of change. In W. R. Miller & S. Rollnick (Eds.), *Motivational interviewing: Preparing people for change* (2nd ed.) (pp. 201–216). New York: The Guilford Press.

Dutton, D. G. (1995). *The domestic assault of women.* Vancouver: UBC Press.

Eisikovits, Z., & Buchbinder, E. (1999). Talking control: Metaphors used by battered women. *Violence Against Women, 5*(8), 845–868.

Erez, E., & Belknap, J. (1998). In their own words: Battered women's assessment of the criminal processing system's response. *Victims and Violence, 13*(3), 251–268.

Fever, C., Meade, L., Milstead, M., & Resick, P. (1999). *The transtheoretical model applied to domestic violence survivors.* Paper presented at the annual meeting of the International Society for Traumatic Stress Studies, Miami, FL.

Fleury, R. E., Sullivan, C. M., & Bybee, D. I. (1998). "Why don't they just call the cops?": Reasons for differential contact among women with abusive partners. *Violence and Victims, 13*(4), 333–346.

Gallant, J. P. (1993). New ideas for the school social worker in the counseling of children and families. *Social Work in Education, 15*(2), 119–125.

Glanz, K., Patterson, R. E., Kristal, A. R., DiClemente, C. C., Heimendinger, J., Linnan, L., & Ockene, J. (1994). Stages of change in adopting healthy diets: Fat, fiber, and correlates of nutrient intake. *Health Education Quarterly, 21*(4), 499–519.

Goodman, M. S., & Fallon, B. C. (1995). *Pattern changes: An educational program for group leaders working with abused and formerly abused women.* Thousand Oaks, CA: Sage.

Griffing, S., Ragin, D. F., Sage, R. E., Madry, L., Bingham, L. E., & Primm, B. J. (2002). Domestic violence survivors' self-identified reasons for returning to abusive relationships. *Journal of Interpersonal Violence, 17*(3), 306–319.

Grimley, D., Prochaska, J. O., Velicer, W. F., Blais, L. M., & DiClemente, C. C. (1994). The transtheoretical model of change. In T. M. Brinthaupt & R. P. Lipka (Eds.), *Changing the self: Philosophies, techniques and experiences* (pp. 201–227). Albany, New York: State University of New York Press.

Hadley, S. M., Short, L. M., Legin, N., & Zook, E. (1995). Womankind: An innovative model of healthcare response to domestic abuse. *Women's Health Issues, 5,* 189–198.

Johnson, V. E. (1986). *Intervention: How to help those who don't want help.* Minneapolis, MN: Johnson Institute.

Kalmuss, D. S., & Straus, M. A. (1982). Wife's marital dependency and wife abuse. *Journal of Marriage and the Family, 44,* 277–286.

Katz, S., & Florian, V. (1986). A comprehensive theoretical model of psychological reaction to loss. *The International Journal of Psychiatry in Medicine, 16*(4), 325–345.

Koss, P. M., Goodman, L. S., Browne, A., Fitzgerald, L. F., Kerta, G. P., & Russo, N. R. (1994). *No safe haven: Male violence against women at home, at work and in the community.* Washington, DC: American Psychological Association.

Lerman, L. G. (1981). *Prosecution of spouse abuse: Innovations in criminal justice response.* Washington, DC: Center for Women Policy Studies.

Lerner, C. F., & Kennedy, L. T. (2000). Stay-leave decision making in battered women: Trauma, coping and self-efficacy. *Cognitive Therapy & Research, 24*(2), 215–232.

Marcus, B. H., Rossi, J. S., Selby, V. C., Niaura, R. S., & Abrams, D. B. (1992). The stages and processes of exercise adoption and maintenance in a worksite sample. *Health Psychology, 11*(6), 386–395.

McConnaughy, E. A., Prochaska, J. O., & Velicer, W. F. (1983). Stages of change in psychotherapy: Measurement and sample profiles. *Psychotherapy: Theory, Research and Practice, 20*(3), 368–375.

McConnaughy, E. A., DiClemente, C. C., Prochaska, J. O., & Velicer, W. F. (1989). Stages of change in psychotherapy: A follow-up report. *Psychotherapy, 26*(4), 494–503.

Mills, L. G. (1998). Mandatory arrest and prosecution policies for domestic violence: Critical literature review and the case for more research to test victim empowerment. *Criminal Justice and Behavior, 25*(3), 306–318.

Mills, L. G. (1999). Killing her softly: Intimate abuse and the violence of state intervention. *Harvard Law Review, 113*(2), 551–613.

Moore, R. B. (1998). Racism in the English language. In P. Rothenberg (Eds.), *Race, class and gender in the United States* (4th ed.) (pp. 465–475). New York: St. Martin's Press.

Morrison, J. (1995). *DSM-IV made easy: The clinician's guide to diagnosis.* New York: Guilford Press.

Morton, E., Runyan, C. W., Moracco, K. E., & Butts, J. (1998). Partner homicide-suicide involving female homicide victims. A population based study in North Carolina, 1988–1992. *Victims & Violence, 13*(2), 91–106.

Pagelow, M. D. (1981). *Women battering: Victims and their experiences.* Beverly Hills, CA: Sage.

Pagelow, M. D. (1984). *Family violence.* New York: Praeger.

Para, E. B., Arkowitz, H., Hannah, M. T., & Vasquez, A. M. (1995). Coping strategies and emotional reactions to separation and divorce in Anglo, Chicana, and Mexicana women. *Journal of Divorce and Remarriage, 23*(1/2), 117–129.

Peled, E., Eisikovits, Z., Enosh, G., & Winstok, Z. (2000). Choice and empowerment for battered women who stay: Toward a constructivist model. *Social Work, 45*(1), 9–25.

Prochaska, J. O. (1996). A stage paradigm for integrating clinical and public health approaches to smoking cessation. *Addictive Behaviors, 21*(6), 721–732.

Prochaska, J. O., Norcross, J. C., & DiClemente, C. C. (2002). *Changing for good: A revolutionary six-stage program for overcoming bad habits and moving your life positively forward.* New York: Harper Collins Publishers.

Rinfret-Raynor, M., Paqnet-Deeby, A., Larouche, G., & Cantin, S. (1992). Intervening with battered women: Evaluating the effectiveness of a feminist model. *National Clearinghouse on Family Violence of Health and Welfare,* Canada.

Rusbult, C. E., & Martz, J. M. (1995). Remaining in an abusive relationship: An investment model analysis of nonvoluntary dependence. *Personality & Social Psychology Bulletin, 21*(6), 558–571.

Ryan, R. M., Plant, R. W., & O'Malley, S. (1995). Initial motivation for alcohol treatment: Relations with patient characteristics, treatment involvement and dropout. *Addictive Behaviors, 20*(3), 279–297.

Saleebey, D. (Ed.). (1997). *The strengths perspective in social work practice* (2nd ed.). New York: Longman, Inc.

Shulman, L. (1992). *The skills of helping: Individuals, families, and groups* (3rd ed.). Itasca, IL: F. E. Peacock Publishers.

Simerly, D. E. (1996). Time for a change: Prediction of a woman's return to her batterer. *Dissertation Abstracts International, 56*(11-B), 6447. (UMI No. 04194217)

Simpson, D. D., & Joe, G. W. (1993). Motivation as a predictor of early dropout from drug abuse treatment. *Psychotherapy, 30,* 357–368.

Smith, A. (2001). Domestic violence laws: The voices of battered women. *Violence and Victims, 16*(1), 91–111.

Smith, E. D., & Gray, C. (1995). Integrating and transcending divorce: A transpersonal model. *Social Thought, 18*(1), 57–74.

Smith, S., Williams, M. B., & Rosen, K. (Eds.). (1990). *Violence hits home: Comprehensive treatment approaches to domestic violence.* New York: Springer Publishing Company.

Stackman, D. K. (1997). Factors influencing whether or not women return to their abusive partners: Psychological effect of battering and women's connection with others regarding their abusive experiences. *Dissertation Abstracts International, 58*(1-B), 0429. (UMI No. 04194217)

Sullivan, C. M., & Alexy, C. (2001). *Outcome evaluation strategies for domestic violence service programs: A practical guide.* National Resource Center on Domestic Violence.

Supplemental Security Income Modernization Project (1992). *Final report of the experts.* Baltimore, MD: SSI Modernization Project.

Tolson, E. R., Reid, W. J., & Garvin, C. D. (2003). *Generalist practice: A task-centered approach* (3rd ed). New York: Columbia University Press.

Totman, J. (1978). *The murderess: A psychosocial study of criminal homicide.* San Francisco: R & E Research Associates.

Ucko, L. G. (1991). Who's afraid of the big bad wolf? Confronting wife abuse through folk stories. *Social Work, 36*(5), 414–419.

Walker, L., & Meloy, J. R. (1998). Stalking and domestic violence. In J. R. Meloy (Ed.), *The psychology of stalking: Clinical and forensic perspectives* (pp. 139–161). San Diego, CA: Academic Press, Inc.

Wells, M. T. (1998). *Assessing battered women's readiness to change: An instrument development study.* Paper presented at annual meeting of the International Society for Traumatic Stress Studies, Washington, DC.

Witvliet, C. V., Ludwig, T. E., & Vander Laan, K. L. (2001). Granting forgiveness or harboring grudges: Implications for emotion, physiology, and health. *Psychological Science, 121*(2), 117–123.

3

Betty and Charlie Bristol

Shelley Schuurman

Introduction

The school day was off to a good start. The twelve emotionally impaired special education students were all on task. This upper elementary self-contained classroom was often the noisiest in the school. Many of the boys, and they were all boys, came from chaotic and unpredictable home environments. Keeping the boys on task presented a challenge, but Mrs. May was up for it. She cared about her students and it seemed the feeling was mutual.

Charlie, an eleven-year-old boy full of energy, raised his hand and asked to sharpen his pencil. Mrs. May said yes. She also praised Charlie for remembering to ask before bolting over to the pencil sharpener, his usual style. Not three minutes later he asked again, this time in a loud and demanding voice. Mrs. May, again, praised Charlie for asking but reminded him that he had just sharpened his pencil minutes ago. Charlie began to shift in his seat, raise his voice, and demand that he sharpen his pencil, NOW!

Mrs. May came over to his seat to speak to him and he lashed at her with his pencil. Trying to dodge the pencil's sharp point, she quickly backed away, stumbling over a book on the floor. The next thing she remembered, Mrs. May was lying on the ground. Seconds later, she felt the crushing blow of a shoe connecting with her nose. She winced and tried to cover her face, but another forceful kick connected with her right ear. After several more blows to the ear, the room went black.

Professional Systems Mobilize

Within moments, several professionals gathered outside the classroom door. School personnel detained Charlie in a locked seclusion room. Mrs. May was recovering in another classroom, waiting for the police to arrive before going to the hospital. The school principal wondered if Mrs. May needed to press charges or if the school could press charges on her behalf. He had called the police who told him a cruiser was coming.

Next, the school social worker arrived. She questioned whether pressing charges was necessary. She stated that she had been working with Charlie's family for several years and Charlie was simply a product of his environment. His father had been in and out of jail for substance abuse–related charges and she suspected domestic violence in the home. The local Community Mental Health (CMH) agency provided in-home services to the family. The school social worker believed that they currently had an open case. She called CMH for confirmation. CMH paged the family's home-based therapist, who headed directly to the school.

Within minutes, Betty Bristol, Charlie's mother, arrived. Betty was distraught when she heard her son crying in the locked seclusion room. She demanded to see him. Two police officers and the home-based therapist walked in as the principal debated about what to do next. Linda, the home-based therapist from Community Mental Health (CMH), approached Betty and they began talking. Linda explained that Betty would be putting herself in danger by going into the seclusion room. Linda reminded Betty of her worries about being unable to control Charlie at home. Betty knew Charlie could become aggressive but insisted that she managed him well.

The police officer interrupted the two women to relay the information that Mrs. May decided to press charges. The officer informed Betty that the police charged Charlie with assault and battery. The police officer offered to transfer Charlie to detention, if Mrs. Bristol did not feel safe taking him home. She agreed.

Betty was overwhelmed. She felt as if her life was coming apart at the seams and she could not stop it. Where did she go wrong? How could this be happening? She tried to do the right thing, love her husband, take good care of her children; it wasn't supposed to turn out like this.

Our First Meeting

Three weeks later, I met Betty Bristol and her son, Charlie Bristol. CMH and the juvenile court referred them for an intake assessment at the secure residential treatment facility where I work. I am the therapist for the eight-to-twelve-year-old boys' program in the facility's large multi-faceted youth services.

I received their paperwork prior to the appointment and spoke with the CMH worker assigned to their case. Their file states that Charlie was impulsive, verbally and physically aggressive, manipulative, anxious, disruptive in school; experienced nightmares; did not comply with limits set by parents; lied frequently; and destroyed property. The CMH worker also stated that Charlie needed residential placement. She considered him a threat to his home and community. The CMH worker's information about the Bristol family listed suspected domestic violence. Mr. Bristol, Charlie's father, had a history of substance abuse and frequent incarcerations for related charges. Mrs. Bristol was uneducated and unwilling to leave her abusive husband or control her children.

The CMH worker also called to speak with me prior to the intake assessment. She reported that the Bristol family had been in their system for years and that the parents were "beyond hope." She said that Mr. Bristol was a violent alcoholic that refused treatment. Betty had attended therapy for herself and her children but was resistant to change and unwilling to leave a very dangerous relationship with her husband. The CMH worker believed that Betty was more "invested" in her dysfunctional relationship with her husband than properly caring for her children. The worker said that Betty, by staying in her relationship, had continually put her children at risk. The worker recommended that I "forget" about the parents since their parental rights would probably end in the near future. She suggested I focus treatment on the children.

I hung up the phone and contemplated our conversation, trying to make sense of it. I could understand burnout and I know the patience and persistence it takes to work with difficult cases. However, this worker's lack of hope for this family and her apparent anger towards them struck me. If she had no hope, how could she instill hope in the family? She labeled Betty's inability to leave her abusive husband as "resistance." However, I questioned what other hopeful options she presented to Betty as realistic solutions. Family therapy research indicates repeatedly that a client's relationship with their therapist is the key factor in determining positive treatment outcomes. Bergin and Garfield (1994), along with Lambert and Bergin (1994) (cited in Hanna & Brown, 2004), state,

> Repeated studies show that 40 percent of the variance in psychotherapy outcome is related to client attributes and factors outside the therapy process, 30 percent is related to the therapeutic relationship, 15 percent is related to the client's sense of hope, and another 15 percent is related to specific techniques and models of the therapist. Thus amid this formula for success, increasing the sense of hope is an important function of the therapeutic relationship (pp. 96–97).

I wondered about Betty's hopes and dreams and became determined to ignore the CMH worker's negative assumptions about her and the family. I invited this family into my office, ready to look at their situation through fresh eyes.

Questions

Having not met the family, the author presented information about Charlie and the Bristol family from the case records of their former therapist. It appeared that their former therapist had strong negative opinions about this family and their hope for the future. She even suggested that Betty was "invested" in being abused. Many practitioners and students believe that people "like" or "need" their problems and do not want to give them up. In this case, apparently, Betty would rather be abused than care for her children. Given the infor-

mation learned to this point, answer the following questions before moving ahead with this case.

1. What is your first hunch regarding the presenting problem? Explore the practice literature and discuss your ideas. What does the practice literature say about children who attack authority figures in the way Charlie attacked Mrs. May? If the literature does not speak specifically about this problem, are there other problems or categories of problems that this behavior fits with pertaining to treatment?

2. What is the next direction of inquiry and assessment? Further, explore the practice literature to locate theories or models that apply to this type of behavior in young boys. Based on the approaches you find, what information would you need to collect to perform a comprehensive and/or multi-systemic assessment? (See Chapter 1.)

3. What personal strengths can you locate and name at this early juncture in treatment?

4. Explore the literature; use your experiences and the experience of others to consider the CMH worker's comments about the family. If you were the therapist, what issues would you address to engage this family in treatment? Explain your ideas and discuss them with classmates.

Building Rapport

When we met, Betty appeared small and young. She looked as much like a child as her eleven-year-old son did. She appeared tired and worn-out, though her jaw was clenched with a hint of determination. Charlie, on the other hand, was full of energy and eager to explore the toys I placed on the table.

I asked Charlie why he thought he was here and he replied, "Because of my anger." I asked him what he was angry about and he shrugged his shoulders, "I don't know." He said that he gets mad sometimes and hurts people. Charlie said that he had just "hurt his teacher."

He lowered his eyes and looked ashamed. I asked him if he would like help learning how to control his anger. Charlie nodded. He then said that he did not want to go to jail like his dad. I asked if his dad went to jail for hurting people and he said no, his dad went to jail for too much drinking. Charlie worried about going to jail after talking to someone from "kid's jail" because of what he did to his teacher. I asked Charlie if he had any ideas about what might work to help him control his anger. He said nothing helps.

Charlie felt sorry for his actions and always apologizes, but he always seems to do it again. I asked if he thought it might be okay to stay here (residential center) for a while so he can get help. Charlie looked at his mom and then at me and said, "I guess . . . if it's okay with my mom."

Betty said she wanted to think about it and asked if she could speak to me privately. I found someone to supervise Charlie. Betty and I left the room. She shared that she was having trouble controlling him and that he had seriously hurt his teacher. Betty knew that Charlie needed help with his anger. She also stated that she was reluctant to leave him in a residential program. As a mother myself, I empathized and said that it would be difficult for me to leave one of my children in a residential setting, as well. She talked about her other two children, ages thirteen and eight. I shared that I had two sons who were twenty and seventeen. Betty stated that her other children seemed "fine." Charlie was the child giving her the most difficulty.

I chose to share this personal information about myself because I find the "use of self as a therapist" an effective component in rapport building with clients. Moreover, I find it easy to share snippets of my life when it helps the relationship and it fits within the theoretical framework from which I work. I admire the work of Virginia Satir and describe my "therapeutic style" or way that I approach the therapeutic relationship in terms of her theory. Satir (1987) said it well when she wrote,

> When the emphasis is totally on empowering the patient, the therapist will tend to choose methods that serve that purpose. When therapists work at empowering, the patient is more likely to have opportunities to experience old attitudes in new contexts. They have the experience of interacting with their therapist; of getting, in addition to, giving feedback. The treatment context becomes a life-learning and life-giving context between the patient and a therapist, who responds personally and humanly. The therapist is clearly identified as a self interacting with another self. Within this context, the therapist's use of self is the main tool for change. Using self, the therapist builds trust and rapport so more risks can be taken. The use of self by the therapist is an integral part of the therapeutic process and it should be used consciously for treatment purposes (p. 23).

Questions

As longtime practitioners and social work educators, the editors find that what, when, if, and how much practitioners should share about their lives with clients always generates interesting dialogue and debate. Some believe that sharing personal information is a way of joining clients as well as being genuine in the relationship. Others believe that practitioners should not share personal information with clients under any circumstances. This interesting debate is relevant in every aspect of practice.

1. Explore the practice literature about client engagement, relationship building, and practitioner use of self in practice. Explore these topics either alone or in the context of two or three different theoretical approaches of interest. What does the literature say about professional use of self, defined as sharing personal information with clients? If there are differences between

approaches or models, how do authors account for their beliefs about this issue?

2. **Explore the code of professional ethics (NASW, 2000). What does the code say, if anything, about this issue? List the various standards that might inform practitioners about this issue and come to a decision about its ethicality in practice.**

3. **If you decide that it is appropriate to share personal information, when and under what circumstances is it appropriate?**

4. **If you decide that it is inappropriate to share personal information, explain and defend your position.**

5. **Discuss this issue with classmates. Perhaps, you could have a formal debate in class about this issue as part of your research and decision-making process.**

As Betty and I continued chatting about our children, I brought the conversation back to her fear of leaving Charlie in our residential treatment center. I offered a tour of the facilities. As we walked the grounds, Betty observed that it seemed "homier" than she expected. I asked about her expectations. Betty said that as an adolescent, she lived in a state psychiatric facility for two years and it was a "terrifying" experience. She did not want Charlie to live through the same thing.

Betty's Personal History

As we talked, Betty told me the story of her mother's depression and repeated suicide attempts throughout Betty's childhood. Betty's mother eventually committed suicide when Betty was eleven years old. Shortly after her mother's death, Betty's father began sexually abusing her, the only child in the family. As the abuse progressed, Betty began getting into trouble by running away, skipping school, and "acting crazy." Eventually, youth authorities placed her in a psychiatric institution. She had not seen her father since, and she never reported his abuse to authorities or her therapists at the psychiatric hospital.

Betty lived in the psychiatric institution until she was seventeen. When she left the institution, she met Jerry at a party. He was a "serious partier" already, but so was Betty. Within one year, she became pregnant and married Jerry. Betty was eighteen years old and fresh out of several years living in an institution after living with her father's sexual abuse, and Jerry was twenty when they were married. Over the years, Jerry developed a problem with drinking and had frequently been to jail for driving under the influence and other assorted alcohol-related offenses. She said that Jerry, his father, and two younger brothers were also problem drinkers. She also mentioned that Jerry's father was a violent man, abusing his wife and sons over the years. Jerry often says that he is still afraid of his father when he is drunk.

According to Betty, Jerry worked construction sometimes but had trouble making enough money to "make ends meet." The family relied on welfare, specifically food stamps and Medicaid, to get by. Though she knew that "things aren't ideal," she was proud of remaining married to the same man for thirteen years, despite his problems. She talked with genuine pride about her two children and said they meant the "world" to her.

I suggested to Betty that I sensed how important her family was and how exhausted she was. I empathized with her about the difficulty she must have parenting Charlie. I emphasized that I believed that residential placement at this time, given the circumstances of Charlie's attack on his teacher, might be in his best interest. I vowed that we could provide Charlie and her family with the help they needed at this time. I explained the benefits of intensive counseling in a residential setting and added that I thought she would also benefit from some relief from his disruptive behavior.

Moving Toward Engagement

Betty was becoming comfortable admitting Charlie to our program. Her major concern pertained to the CMH worker. Betty feared that if she left Charlie with us, the CMH therapist would not "let her" have Charlie back. She said, "I know she doesn't like me . . . she doesn't think I'm a good enough mother because of how Jerry acts." When I asked her why CMH believed that, she said that her husband hit her "occasionally," but he was always sorry. Besides, Betty said, "Jerry wasn't doing it as much as he used to." Betty also said that she would never let him hurt the kids and that he never hit them, only her.

I empathized with Betty, expressing my understanding about how difficult it must be in her situation. If Charlie entered our program, I would become his primary therapist and would be responsible for making recommendations about his living arrangements after he completed the program. I assured Betty that I thought home was the best place for a child, as long as it was a safe and healthy environment. I suggested to Betty that she and I could work together to make her home this kind of place. We talked about her participating in individual and family therapy. I expressed my concern about her safety and that we would need to explore this issue soon. Betty agreed to our plan and admitted Charlie into our program. Betty further agreed to attend weekly family and individual therapy. We decided to begin family therapy with her and Charlie, hoping to involve Jerry soon.

Questions

Now that the author has presented more information about Betty and Charlie, and before reading her assessment and diagnoses below, perform this exercise based on your education, experience, the professional literature, and best-practices evidence. To increase the learning potential of this exercise, you may want to do this in a small group with other students in your course.

1. Based on the information provided, construct a three-generation genogram and eco-map that represent Betty and Charlie's personal, familial,

and environmental circumstances. What further information do you need to complete this exercise? What patterns do these two important graphical assessment tools demonstrate?

2. Building on the list you began earlier, complete a list of their issues and strengths.

3. Write a two- to three-page narrative assessment that encompasses Betty and Charlie's multi-systemic issues and strengths. Review Chapter 1 if needed. This narrative should provide a comprehensive and multi-systemic explanation of their lives as they prepare to undergo therapy with the author.

4. Identify the theoretical model or approach that you use to guide your assessment. According to the literature, what other theoretical options are available, and how would these change the nature of your assessment?

5. End by developing multi-axial DSM-IV-TR diagnoses for both Betty and Charlie. Be sure to look for evidence of multiple diagnoses on Axis I. Provide the list of client symptoms that you used to justify your diagnostic decisions. What, if any, information were you missing that would make this an easier task?

6. What effect did working from a secure residential placement have on your assessment and later treatment methods? Did Charlie's court-ordered status have any effect on your thinking? Explain your answers.

7. Did you have enough information to complete these exercises? If not, make a list of the information you would need to complete each exercise.

First Session Review

After helping Charlie settle into the program and saying good-bye to Betty, I returned to my office and reflected on the intake session. I mulled over my impressions of the Bristol family with whom I would now be working for months to come. I felt good about my "connection" with Betty and pleased that she shared detailed and personal information. She must have felt comfortable. I was impressed that she admitted Jerry's physical abuse and her history of sexual abuse, especially since she never told her other therapists. I interpreted this as a positive indicator of engagement.

I believe that the more I can connect with clients at intake, the greater the likelihood of a successful treatment outcome. Hence, I treat the intake assessment as more than a "fact-finding mission." I believe the first meeting is an intervention. When discussing the use of a strengths-based assessment, Graybeal (2001) writes, "Though typically seen as distinct phases of practice, it is critically important to understand that there is not, and cannot be, a distinction made between assessment and intervention" (p. 235). I work especially hard at preparing for assessments. I spend time thinking about the information provided by other professionals and develop my own hypothesis. My hypothesis provides the basis for our first session.

As I mentioned earlier, one of the issues that struck me about the Bristol family was the hostility of the referring CMH therapist. I could feel her negativity, and I wondered how that affected the family's desire to build a relationship with her. As I considered Betty's relationship with the CMH system, I also thought of the other outside systems the family interacted with in their lives. I considered what impact this might have on Betty's desire to connect with yet another system. CMH treated Betty poorly and her memory of the state psychiatric facility was negative. I knew that I had to treat her differently for therapy to succeed.

From the information I received from CMH and Betty, I surmised that the family was interacting not only within its own system but also with at least five other larger systems. They had frequent interaction with the school system because of Charlie's disruptive behavior. This relationship faltered following Charlie's attack on Mrs. May. Charlie also met the juvenile justice system since Mrs. May filed formal charges over the assault. The juvenile justice system was funding 50 percent of the cost of his residential treatment. A probation officer would soon be assigned to the case and work closely with the family and me. Further, CMH referred the family to our agency. CMH had provided services for the past several years. This relationship appeared hostile as evidenced by my conversation with the referring worker.

Finally, Betty shared that the family interacted with the welfare system in order to buy food and have access to health care services and with the adult legal system about Jerry's repeated law violations. I wondered if Betty was sick of having so many systems and agencies involved in her life. I also wondered how it might feel to be Betty right now, meeting yet another "helping professional." From experience, I am aware of the complexities and frustrations involved with getting a large group of professionals to agree on the best course of action for a family. I would not blame Betty for not wanting to add yet another system to the mix. Goldenberg and Goldenberg (2004) state,

> Family systems interact with larger outside systems, such as the church, schools, or the health care system, and the unbending rules of some institutions may negate any therapeutic gain. Although these systems are often effective in solving problems, in a sizable number of cases confusion may result from competing definitions of the family problem and conflicting solutions offered by different helpers in this macrosystem (p. 91).

My job was to navigate the various systems carefully to ensure the Bristol family was receiving the services they needed and that all involved parties worked in the family's best interest. I attempted to engage Betty about this issue by assuring her that once Charlie entered the program, I would become the primary therapist, coordinating all other involved parties.

Human Diversity and Cultural Competency

Two areas of human diversity stood out to me as I worked with the Bristol family. The first was gender. It was clear to me that the CMH worker framed Betty's inability to leave her abusive husband as resistance. This person's lack of knowledge regarding gender differences, domestic violence, codependency, and societal oppression of women in marriage bordered on cultural incompetence and, at the very least, impeded any possible treatment progress. Hanna and Brown (2004) discuss the issue of perceived resistance in the following way:

> In family therapy, there is a strong bias toward the notion that resistance is an interactional event characterized by the professional's lack of understanding about what is important to the family. For example, battered women are often considered resistant when they fail to follow professional advice that places physical safety above psychological safety. While there is a widespread agreement about the importance of physical safety as a human right, professionals are frequently guilty of blaming the innocent when they label clients as resistant or stubborn without understanding the history that has influenced their beliefs about self, others and the world around them (p. 98).

In my role of practitioner, I tried to respect Betty's need to decide about her marriage in her own time. I withheld my assumptions about why she was unprepared to leave Jerry at this time. Instead, we explored with her the possible dangers that she and her children may encounter by staying. I acknowledged gender differences in the need for "connectedness" in relationships and considered the real limitations of many women's access to social and financial resources.

The second area of diversity is socioeconomic status. The Bristol family fit in the category of the "working poor." The chronic stress associated with poverty and class is a significant stressor (Johnson, 2004) that affects Betty's decision-making process. Not only was she exhausted by the daily tasks of paying the bills and parenting children with special needs, she had to consider how she and her children would survive financially if she left her current living arrangement. Betty did not graduate from high school and had been unemployed outside the home for several years. I imagined that she felt overwhelmed by even considering the possibility of divorce, given her socioeconomic status.

Moreover, Betty was a survivor of childhood sexual abuse and domestic violence in her marriage. These issues would play a central role in our work together and often represent a constellation of beliefs and values about self and others that play a significant role in client willingness to engage in therapy as well as leave her abusive marriage. Abused women tend to leave and return to physically violent relationships several times before permanently leaving (Stackman, 1997, cited in Black & Shelly, 2005).

Rusbult and Martz (1995, cited in Black & Shelly, 2005) found that a sense of commitment to the relationship was important when determining whether women would leave their abusive partners. Betty expressed pride in remaining married to Jerry for thirteen years. Moreover, married women with few economic choices tend to remain longer in abusive relationships. Some women permanently leave abusive relationships, some continue to leave and return, and others choose to stay with abusive partners. Abused women stay with their partners for many reasons, including financial dependence, concern for children, pressure from family, fear of retaliation from partner, and emotional attachment to partner. In fact, research suggests that abused women are at greater risk of harm by leaving than staying (Mills, 1998, cited in Black & Shelly, 2005).

No therapy could be successful without making these issues central to the process for Betty and Charlie. After all, Charlie grew up watching his father beat his mother whenever he wanted. It is little wonder that Charlie attacked people too.

My strategy for demonstrating cultural competence was to remain aware of my expectations and not thrust them onto Betty. Rather, my job was to listen to her story as she told it and ask for clarification in an effort to understand her worldview and beliefs about her life and future. As a clinician, I've seen change or movement towards health occur when clients feel heard, genuinely understood, and cared for. Edward Teyber (2000) wrote,

> Therapists must actively extend themselves to the client and directly express their feeling and concern for the client. That is, therapists must articulate the understanding of the client's experience in a way that also communicates their compassion and care for the client (p. 42).

Questions

Before moving on, compare your assessment to the author's. Where do you find points of agreement and disagreement? Discuss these issues with classmates and use the professional literature to analyze the differences.

1. What implications for treatment arise because of the differences you discovered between the author's assessment and your assessment?

2. Explain these differences as part of a treatment plan. That is, develop a treatment plan for Charlie and Betty based on your assessment. Include the types of treatment, theoretical models, and how these differ from those used by the author.

3. Similar to the exercises above, what effect did Charlie's placement in a secured setting have on treatment and intervention planning? Would you approach this case differently because of the setting versus a traditional outpatient or in-home setting? Explain.

Treatment and Intervention Planning

Before developing a treatment plan for the Bristol family, I considered many issues. First, I considered the amount of time I would have to work with this family. Both referring agencies assured me that I had six months to one year. Knowing the time-frame affected my methods, I knew that I did not have to find a "quick fix" and could spend quality time on relationship building.

Next, I considered the referring workers' reasons for placing Charlie in a secure residential program. I wondered about the agency's desired outcomes. I consulted with the CMH worker and Charlie's probation officer to clarify these issues. I needed to incorporate their goals into the treatment plan, since they were responsible for funding his placement.

I also considered the diversity issues of gender, socioeconomic status, childhood sexual abuse, and domestic violence in my planning. Hence, I planned treatment in ways that I felt were sensitive to Betty and addressed her main issues. I always consider personal safety in assessment, treatment planning, and treatment. With this case, Betty lived with the constant threat of domestic violence. Therefore, I developed a safety plan for Betty.

Finally, I considered the issue of substance abuse. On a case-by-case basis, I try to decide whether I can address it or whether I need to refer out to a substance abuse therapist. I decided to refer Jerry Bristol out for substance abuse treatment. I provide my rationale for this decision later.

I completed the treatment plan three weeks after initially meeting with Betty and Charlie. Hence, I considered several things that transpired at the Bristol home during this time. The CMH worker was continuing in-home treatment with Betty and the other two children. CMH set a condition that Betty had to seek a court-order removing Jerry from the family home or have the children removed. The CMH worker did not believe Betty and Jerry followed the order and remained worried about Betty and her children's safety. The CMH worker told Betty that if she was allowing Jerry into the home, she was placing her children at risk and Child Protective Services (CPS) would remove them from her care. The CMH worker also told me Jerry requested permission to visit Charlie.

Questions

Let's set the stage. The local CMH and juvenile court referred Charlie and Betty to the residential unit for treatment that included family therapy. Yet, according to the author, the CMH worker continued performing in-home family therapy with Betty and her other children, despite the worker's obvious hostility toward Betty and Jerry. While the author performed family therapy aimed at helping the family, the CMH worker took steps to dissolve the family through a court order and threats. Regardless of whether you believe Betty should leave Jerry at this point, think about the issue of multiple helping systems working with the same family in therapy.

1. Explore the literature and best-practices evidence to see if anyone has written about this issue and its effect on eventual clinical outcome. What does

the literature say about the efficacy of multiple systemic involvements in the same case?

2. Explore the practices of the various systems in your state or county. What are their policies regarding situations such as this? Dialogue with classmates about this issue to discover what happens in practice where you live.

3. Based on your inquiry, list the issues raised by having two therapists in this family's life at the same time. Is it possible for two different therapists to perform family therapy separately and have a positive outcome? If so, explain your answer in detail.

4. Based on your inquiry and experience, does this scenario present barriers to or opportunities for successful treatment outcome? Explain your answers.

5. In the context of the latest literature about domestic violence, determine what effect the CMH worker's insistence on a court order removing Jerry from the house might have on treatment.

Theories and Methods of Family Therapy

My next step was to consider which family therapy models and/or interventions would be most effective with the family. There is little direction or guidance on this topic in the current social work practice literature. It seems to me that most therapists have a specific model or theory they use most of the time. Consequently, therapists develop treatment plans according to the specifics of their favorite model or theory. The family therapy field offers several models of practice. Many can be effective with families such as the Bristol family. Hence, it is important that practitioners not follow one model at the expense of the others.

I do not formulate treatment plans based on one particular school of thought or way of thinking about families. Instead, my primary focus is the collaborative therapeutic relationship I develop with the family. I try to set this tone in the initial assessment, verbalizing the importance of the family and I working together to solve the problems that brought them to treatment. Teyber (2000) suggests that "clients cannot resolve problems and achieve a greater sense of their own personal power in a hierarchical or one up/one down therapeutic relationship" (p. 31). All of the children and families I worked with are survivors of physical, sexual, or emotional abuse where they lived in a perpetual "one down" position in relationships. Knowing this, I find it even more important to establish a working alliance with clients where together we discuss treatment goals and devise objectives to accomplish them.

As I stated earlier, my primary therapeutic style is most similar to Carl Rogers or Virginia Satir. Virginia was an advocate for the strengths-based approach before anyone called it such. For example,

The "love" she practiced with clients and that she postulated as a necessary condition for actualizing one's capabilities was based on her assumptions about what best facilitates change. Satir assumed people were whole, authentic, sensitive, and genuine with one another. Thus, she looked for and found in people signs of their healthy intentions, even when these behaviors were embedded in unhealthy behavior (Lawrence, 1999, cited in Goldenberg & Goldenberg, 2004, p. 170).

With this being my primary style, my next step is to conceptualize the overriding areas of concern and explore what models or theories best address these issues. As I considered the specific issues in the Bristol family, I believed that the domestic violence was the primary cause of each family member's distress. I reread the literature on trauma and Posttraumatic Stress Disorder (PTSD) and formulated possible treatment goals that I thought might be effective. I also outlined interventions taken from various models of family therapy that contained a variety of treatment modalities.

Next, I met with each family member individually and explored the issues each wanted to work on. I shared what I thought the overriding problems were and the ideas I had to assist the family in addressing them. Together everyone agreed on the specifics. We put the following treatment plan in place for the first three months of Charlie's care:

Treatment Plan for Bristol Family

Problem: Frequent acts of physical aggression by Charlie

Goal: Decrease acts of physical aggression by Charlie

Objective: Charlie will increase his self-awareness of what's happening just prior to his acting-out episodes.

Intervention: Therapist will provide a safe and trusting environment where Charlie can begin to recognize and express his feelings.

Intervention: Therapist will assist Charlie in recognizing how his different affective states feel in his body.

Objective: Charlie will learn self-soothing techniques.

Intervention: Therapist will teach relaxation and self-soothing techniques.

Intervention: Therapist will refer Charlie to Affect-Regulation Group.

Problem: Chaotic and violent family environment

Goal: Obtain a structured and safe family environment

Objective: Betty will recognize the dangers of continuing a relationship with Jerry.

Intervention: Therapist will refer Betty to a Women's Survivor Support Group.

Intervention: Therapist will provide a safe and trusting environment where Betty can begin to explore issues surrounding domestic violence.

Intervention: Therapist will make a safety plan with Betty.

Objective: Betty and Charlie will demonstrate healthy parent-child boundaries.

Intervention: Therapist will meet individually with Betty to explore healthy parenting practices.

Intervention: Therapist will meet individually with Charlie and explore issues of domestic violence, substance abuse and healthy families.

Intervention: Therapist will meet with Betty and Charlie to explore and practice healthy parent-child boundaries.

Problem: Chronic substance abuse and domestic violence issues with Jerry

Goal: Jerry will obtain sobriety and discontinue acts of violence in order to have contact with Charlie.

Objective: Jerry will take ownership of his substance abuse problem.

Intervention: Therapist will refer Jerry to specific Substance Abuse Treatment.

Objective: Jerry will take ownership of his violent/controlling behavior.

Intervention: Jerry will attend Men's Domestic Violence Group.

Objective: After Jerry demonstrates his participation in the above-mentioned groups, he will begin to have supervised speaker phone contact with Charlie.

Questions

1. **Compare the treatment plan you established above with the author's treatment plan. What differences and similarities exist between the plans? How do you account for the differences? Use the professional literature and practice evidence to analyze both plans and the differences between them.**

2. **Develop a revised treatment plan from information provided by the author, your original plan, and the practice literature. What does the evidence-based practice literature say are the most effective ways to treat clients with the Bristols' problems and strengths? Using the rationale from the literature and your experience, develop a position on this issue.**

Rationale

First, we addressed Charlie's frequent acts of physical aggression. This behavior was the reason for Charlie's referral to secure residential treatment, so it seemed the best place to start. Charlie was eager to work on this goal and seemed genuine in his desire to stop physically acting out. I hypothesized that his acts of physical aggression were brought on by a posttraumatic stress response from witnessing repeated acts of domestic violence in his home. When his trauma response triggered, Charlie's ability to modulate his affect appeared almost nonexistent and his immediate response was physical aggression. Bessel A. van der Kolk (1987) states,

> The human response to trauma is relatively constant across traumatic stimuli: the central nervous system seems to react to any overwhelming threatening and uncontrollable experience in a consistent pattern. Regardless of the precipitating event, traumatized people continue to have a poor tolerance for arousal. They tend to respond to stress in an all or nothing way: unmodulated anxiety, often accompanied by motoric discharge that includes acts of aggression against the self or others (p. 64).

With this in mind, the first long-term objective helped Charlie modulate his affect. Since this treatment plan was for the first three months of Charlie's care, I began by helping Charlie increase his awareness of what happened before physically acting out. I also taught Charlie several self-soothing techniques such as visualization and deep breathing.

I addressed this issue in individual and group therapy. Individual therapy allowed me time with Charlie to develop trust so that he was comfortable sharing his feelings. Group therapy provided Charlie a chance to interact with peers in a controlled environment along with opportunities to participate in experiential practice modulating his affect. I also assigned homework to help him practice in the milieu. Being a resident in a residential treatment facility, Charlie also received ongoing behavioral therapy from the youth treatment staff.

Next, we addressed their chaotic and violent home environment. This problem seemed to be at the heart of much of the family's inability to function in a healthy manner. I approached this issue with care, not wanting to alienate Betty. I knew that she felt "put down" by the CHM worker for not leaving Jerry and I did not want her to get that same feeling from me.

Instead of suggesting an objective that asked Betty to leave Jerry, I suggested that she explore the pros and cons of staying with Jerry. I framed her desire to stay with Jerry as potentially dangerous behavior that had a healthy intention. I asked Betty to explore this with me. Initially, Betty hesitated but finally agreed. We decided to meet individually on a weekly basis to talk about this. She was also open to developing a safety plan and attending a Women's Survivor Support Group in her hometown. I believed that the group would be educational and beneficial. It is often helpful to hear from others who have gone through similar experiences. People respond well to support groups because they listen to others with similar experiences, make new social connections, and find people near that they can call in an emergency.

Our second objective entailed working on healthy parent-child boundaries between Betty and Charlie. Betty had clearly lost control of Charlie. She needed to reestablish the appropriate generational boundaries as a first step to regaining parental control over her son. When discussing the treatment of traumatized families, van der Kolk (1987) stated,

> The first phase involves helping the family establish as much safety as is necessary and possible and empowering the responsible adults to gain a modicum of control over the environment. The second phase is a slow reconstruction of the family system accomplished by establishing effective interpersonal and generational boundaries and hierarchies and repairing damaged parent-child and marital dyads (p. 145).

Structural family therapy (Minuchin, 1974) discusses the importance of boundaries and suggests that the parental subsystem needs to function in a healthy manner for the rest of the family to do the same. I chose to address this issue by using psychoeducational materials.

In an article discussing family therapy and psychoeducation, Dinkmeyer (1993) states that "many parent-child relationships and family problems have a common thread. Parents often have no alternatives to their present behaviors. Education plays an effective part in the treatment of family problems" (p.189). I decided it would be best to discuss this topic with Betty and Charlie in their individual sessions, as well as in family sessions.

With Charlie, we began using the workbook *I Wish the Hitting Would Stop: A Workbook for Children Living in Violent Homes* (Patterson, 1990). In my individual sessions with Betty, we focused on material from the book *Healthy Parenting: An Empowering Guide for Adult Children* (Woititz, 1992). In family sessions, Betty practiced setting limits with Charlie and Charlie practiced letting mom be in charge. We talked about parent-child interactions that had taken place in their home and together worked to find healthy alternatives. I also modeled healthy parent-child communication and limit setting with Charlie.

The final problem we addressed in the treatment plan was Jerry's chronic substance abuse and violent behavior in the home. Jerry requested visitation with Charlie, and I needed to decide whether to allow these visits to begin immediately or request that Jerry engage in treatment prior to visitation. I also had to decide whether I could provide this treatment for Jerry.

I decided not to provide the treatment myself. Jerry was not involved in substance abuse treatment or "owning" the domestic violence. I believed that my role as the therapist for two of his "victims" placed me in a conflict of interest. Furthermore, since he had been court ordered out of the home, I believed that my working with him and his family was a conflict of interest. Hence, I referred Jerry to substance abuse treatment and a Men's Domestic Violence Group.

The decision of whether to mandate treatment prior to allowing visitation was difficult. Charlie made frequent requests to see his dad. Despite the violence and chaotic home environment, Charlie appeared attached to his dad and recalled several positive stories about fishing, playing with the dog, and riding go-carts with his dad.

Alternatively, Charlie's frequent acts of physical aggression towards peers and staff in the residential unit often required physical restraint. During these episodes, he became distraught and often screamed and sobbed about the violence he witnessed at home. He also appeared hyperactive-vigilant to stress or discord with peers and would attack staff members intervening with peers, shouting, "Get off her and leave her alone!" These incidents seemed as if they were reenactments at home when Jerry became violent towards Betty.

Questions

The author decided to refer Jerry for treatment outside her agency, believing that it was a conflict of interest to treat him with the rest of his family. Based on your experience and information taken from the practice literature, respond to the following questions.

1. Present both sides of the argument made by the author. That is, explore the literature, your experience, and the experience of classmates and make a case for referring Jerry and for treating Jerry as part of the family. Be mindful that Betty had not willingly left Jerry. He was removed from the home under court order through the CMH worker. Does this change your handling of the issue? Please explain.

2. Further address this issue in the context of the code of ethics (NASW, 2000). What standards address the conflict of interest claim made by the author?

3. If you were the practitioner, what would you do in this instance? Explain your answer.

Making a Decision about Visitation

In individual therapy, Charlie began talking about the fears around his dad's drinking and violent behavior. I was concerned that contact with his dad would interfere with his treatment as Charlie returned to his original stance of defending and protecting his dad. I consulted my supervisor who told me to trust my instincts. My instincts told me to require Charlie's dad to attend treatment before reintroducing him into Charlie's life. My supervisor supported my decision.

I also spoke with the consulting psychiatrist. I trusted her judgment and wanted additional input. I feared that Jerry would probably not follow through with treatment, so it could be a long time before Charlie would see him. I shared this concern with the psychiatrist. She asked me to decide what I believed was in Charlie's best interest. I explained that I thought contact with his dad could interfere with Charlie's progress. She replied, "Then you know what you need to do, don't you?"

Therefore, I decided to put off contact with the dad until, at a minimum, he assumed ownership of his substance abuse and physical battering by beginning treatment. When I phoned Mr. Bristol to inform him of my decision, he verbally assaulted me. He told me that I had no right to keep him from his son and then explained that he did not need treatment for anything. He threatened to come to the facility regardless of my decision (which the judge supported) and visit Charlie.

Jerry used vulgar language and yelled at me. I repeated the requirements for visitation and informed him that I was hanging up the phone. Jerry continued leaving angry messages with me for several days but never followed through on his threat to visit without permission.

When I explained my decision to Charlie, I framed it in terms of each member of the family having to do their part. We talked about Charlie's willingness to work on his self-control and not hitting others, how his mom worked on setting limits and being in charge of the family, and how dad needed to do his part and work on his problems too. I explained that when his dad began doing his part, then we could start the telephone contact. Maybe I just imagined it, but Charlie appeared almost relieved to hear this. He did not contest it in any way or ask to see his dad again for quite some time.

Course of Treatment

I continued working with Betty and Charlie for twelve more months, fifteen months total.

For clarity, I will describe their course of treatment in three-month increments.

Betty

By the end of the first three-month period, Betty and I had developed a significant level of trust. She began to believe that I was her advocate and understood her role as advocate for her children. She confided that she had been letting Jerry stay at their home from time to time. She said his visits were becoming more frequent and he was refusing to leave when she asked him. She knew that if she told me this information, I would have to report it to CPS and they would remove her two other children. I did report this to CPS, and they placed her other two children in temporary foster care near her home.

Betty then made a breakthrough in her treatment. She said that she did not want to be hit anymore or have her children witness her beatings. This, according to Betty, was her top priority. She broached this subject during a conversation about Charlie's aggressive outbursts and the connection to witnessing Jerry beating her. Betty said that she felt confident she could do what was required of her to get her children back.

This became a turning point in Betty's treatment. She became more assertive and confident in her parenting with Charlie and worked hard in family therapy with the agency managing her other two children in foster care.

By the end of the second three-month period, Betty had filed for divorce and requested a Personal Protection Order (PPO) since Jerry continued harassing and threatening her. In individual therapy, I began using Bowen's (1985) model of family therapy. At this time, Betty seemed ready to look at the maladaptive patterns of behavior that she assumed from her family of origin. She identified her patterns of depression and lack of differentiation in her relationships. We discussed Betty's decreasing level of anxiety and the progress she was making in becoming more differentiated herself. She articulated how she was less reactive and better able to think things through before acting. Papero (2000) describes this well when he states,

> Better-differentiated people base decisions and behavior on well-developed sets of internal beliefs and principles that they have thought about carefully and tested in real life situations. Their actions, therefore, tend to be more self-determined and less reflexively reactive to the actions of others (pp. 25–26).

Betty also passed her GED and found a job working at a Day Care Center. In six months, Betty's life had improved considerably. So too did her outlook on her marriage and her willingness to be an abused woman. She was finished with that role in her life.

During the third three-month period, Betty moved into an apartment, with the help of the Women's Center. We continued looking at transgenerational patterns in her family history, and Betty continued to become more autonomous. She also revisited her sexual abuse by her father and found patterns of victimization in her marriage. As Betty gained increasing insight into her behavior, her ability to detach herself from Jerry's continued harassment improved.

We explored ways to increase social support systems in her life. Betty identified a woman in the community as someone she would like to befriend. I hoped that her continuing attendance at the support group would enlarge her social network. This appeared to be working. As her parenting skills improved, Betty was allowed more time alone with him, even taking Charlie out for an entire day.

During the fourth three-month period, Betty stayed weekends in the Family House on campus and Charlie spent the weekends there with her. Youth treatment staff were close by and available to support and give any needed assistance. This was an important step to achieve before Charlie could go on an overnight visit with Betty. We also began joint family therapy with the other two children and their therapist from the foster agency.

Charlie

Charlie, on the other hand, had begun identifying different affective states and increasing his ability to comply with expectations without defiant opposition. Hence, incidents of verbal or physical aggression dropped considerably. Charlie began accepting limits from Betty and even had a playful saying for the change in her parenting style. He would watch out of my office window for her car to pull up for family therapy. When he saw it, he'd exclaim, "Better watch out, my new mom is back in town!"

Charlie made progress demonstrating that he could use words, instead of hands and feet, to let others know what he needed. He also focused on learning positive ways to get attention and interact with his peers. I continued to explore the trauma of witnessing domestic violence, and he practiced ways to self-soothe when he became anxious. I used guided imagery to teach him relaxation techniques and cognitive restructuring techniques to help turn his negative self-talk into positive statements. He began enjoying his improved relationships and positive feedback from staff and peers. Charlie took pride in his improved self-control.

Charlie kept working on his physical aggression and was doing well. During individual therapy, he began processing the divorce and the loss regarding his father's refusal to participate in treatment. Charlie wondered aloud why his dad liked his drinking more than he liked him. I began psychoeducational therapy with Charlie around this issue. We also used this information during joint family therapy sessions.

Jerry

Jerry called me occasionally. He usually started conversations by blaming me for making his wife divorce him and keeping his children from him. During one rare phone call, he expressed sadness about screwing up his life. He even shared that his father had physically abused him as a child and that he knew he needed help with his temper and his drinking. I encouraged him to seek this help and suggested what a wonderful gift his getting treatment would be to his children. He assured me he was going to follow through this time but never did.

Questions

1. **Take a moment to review Betty's and Charlie's progress in treatment. Based on the author's description, the professional literature, and the latest practice evidence, what occurred to account for their progress?**

2. **What was the theoretical approach or combination of approaches that appeared to work best for Betty? Now, consider the same question regarding Charlie.**

3. **Based on the work you have done earlier, what additional intervention(s) would you recommend for Betty? Now, consider the same question for Charlie. Use the literature and latest evidence to justify your recommendations.**

Termination

During the final three-month period, we began the termination process. Betty continued doing well and received a promotion at the Day Care Center. She took

Charlie on overnight home visits and continued attending family therapy. The other children were beginning the termination process as well. All agencies involved with the family met to develop a termination/transition home plan.

It was imperative for Betty and the children to have support services if they were going to live successfully in the community. We decided that Charlie would go home first because he was the neediest and most behaviorally challenged of the children. Once Betty settled into a routine with Charlie, the other children would return home. CMH identified a family therapist, and Charlie and Betty began meeting with him during this period to discuss the transition and begin building a relationship. The Juvenile Court provided a mentor for each of the children that included eight hours per week of paid respite time. This gave the children additional positive attention and Betty time to take care of herself and adjust to parenting three children alone.

During individual therapy, I began processing the upcoming move home with Charlie. He was anxious about it and began acting out more frequently. We continued processing his move, and I reminded him that he would be coming back for therapy with me every other week for six weeks after his discharge. We spent time together telling stories about all the positive changes Charlie had made since coming to treatment.

During this final three-month period, Jerry continued to harass and even stalk Betty. She reported each incident in hopes that he would be arrested. In fact, the police caught Jerry driving drunk on a suspended license when he caused an accident. He crashed his vehicle into two vehicles, injuring the passengers. Jerry fled the scene of the accident, a police chase ensued, and Jerry crashed his car and fled on foot. Police eventually apprehended Jerry. He was sentenced to eight years in prison.

Charlie went home and did well for two weeks. The other children returned home soon thereafter. Charlie struggled with this change and began refusing to follow Betty's directives. I met with the family for follow-up therapy and we discussed the situation. We came up with the idea of increasing Charlie's time with his mentor, as well as having the family therapist come to the home twice a week to support Betty in setting limits with Charlie. This plan was approved and put into place.

One week later, Charlie became physically aggressive, breaking furniture and assaulting Betty and his younger siblings. The CMH staff helped Betty bring Charlie to the residential facility to meet with me. During this meeting, Charlie began tearing my office apart. He also kicked, hit, and spit on me. I restrained him by myself until staff arrived to help. Charlie continued escalating and was placed in a locked seclusion room. At this time, we decided to readmit him to the residential treatment facility on a respite basis to reassess the situation.

Betty went home and continued doing well with her other children. Charlie continued acting out and did not respond to treatment. We decided Charlie would be readmitted to the secure unit for everyone's safety. It appeared that Charlie did not possess the coping skills or tools to regulate his affect. Upon readmission, we decided to place him in a unit with a different therapist.

Evaluation of Practice

My supervisor and I reviewed the treatment process after Charlie was readmitted. We believed that our treatment approach was helpful. We met with Betty and discussed her perceptions. She felt positive about the treatment process and stated it was the first time she had felt respected by a professional. She was proud of the changes in her life and said she had never felt better. She was concerned for Charlie but also felt that he needed to feel the consequences of his behavior while he was young. Betty did not want him to continue this behavior into adulthood. She did not feel safe having him in her care at this time.

Finally, I met with my supervisor to evaluate treatment outcome. I was disappointed that Charlie could not sustain his success. He worked hard at regulating his affect. I hoped he would be successful at home. However, there was hope. He was further down the path in his journey to emotional health than he was fifteen months ago. Even more important, he now had a mother who learned healthy parenting skills and could provide a safe and nurturing environment for him when he was ready to return home. Although he never engaged in treatment, Jerry had to face the consequences of his actions. Maybe prison will be a turning point for him. One never knows.

Questions

The author presented an interesting, partially successful case that involved many issues commonly found in domestic violence cases. Taking a broad view of this case, reevaluate the author's work and your participation through the questions asked throughout the case.

1. Overall, what is your professional opinion of the work performed in this case? As always, refer to the professional literature, practice evidence, your experience, and the experience of classmates when developing your opinion.

2. Based on this review, what additional or alternative approaches could have been used with this case? That is, if you were the practitioner, how would you have approached this case? Please explain and justify your approach.

3. What did this case demonstrate that you could use in other practice settings? List the most important things you learned and how you can use these in your practice career.

Epilogue

As for Betty, I am honored to have walked beside her as she discovered and embraced her true potential. She was a woman of great courage and tenacity. I admire her deep love for her children and her willingness to look at her painful past to help create a bright and hopeful future. She was truly an amazing woman!

Bibliography

Black, C., & Shelly, S. (2005). Mikki's Story. In J. L. Johnson & G. Grant, Jr. (Eds.). *Casebook in domestic violence*. Boston: Allyn and Bacon.

Bowen, M. (1985). *Family therapy in clinical practice*. New York: Jason Aronson.

Goldenberg, I., & Goldenberg, H. (2004). *Family therapy: An overview*. Pacific Grove, CA: Brooks/ Cole.

Graybeal, C. (2001). Strengths-Based Social Work Assessment: Transforming the Paradigm. *The Journal of Contemporary Human Services, 82*(3), 233–241.

Hanna, S., & Brown, J. (2004). *The practice of family therapy: Key elements across the models*. Pacific Grove: Brooks/Cole.

Johnson, J. L. (2004). *Fundamentals of substance abuse practice*. Pacific Grove, CA: Brooks/Cole.

Minuchin, S. (1974). *Families and family therapy*. Cambridge, MA: Harvard University Press.

National Association of Social Workers. (2000). *Code of Ethics of the National Association of Social Workers*. Washington, DC: Author.

Papero, D. V. (2000). Bowen Systems Theory. In Bevilacqua, L., & Dattilio, F. (Eds.), *Comparative treatments for relationship dysfunction* (pp. 25–43). New York: Springer Publishing Company.

Patterson, S. (1990). *I wish the hitting would stop*. Red Flag Green Flag Resources.

Satir, V. (1987). The Therapist Story. In Baldwin, M. & Satir, V. (Eds.), *The use of self in therapy* (pp. 17–25). New York: Hayworth Press.

Teyber, E. (2000). *Interpersonal process in psychotherapy: A relational approach*. Pacific Grove, CA: Brooks/Cole.

van der Kolk, B. (1987). *Psychological trauma*. Washington DC: American Psychiatric Press, Inc.

Woititz, J. (1992). *Healthy parenting: An empowering guide for adult children*. New York: Simon & Schuster.

4

Faith Harper

Kim Wetterman & Heidi Weipert

Introduction

The domestic violence agency where I worked as a case manager typically did not deal with cases such as the one I describe in this chapter. The uniqueness of this case caused excitement and trepidation for everyone. Whenever a new client arrived at the shelter, a flurry of activity surrounded them. Yet, this case became more compelling than any other I had worked with in the past. As Faith Harper's story unfolded, the complexities seemed overwhelming. No one knew where to begin, or what to do. Working with Faith changed me as a social worker, in unexpected ways. It introduced me to the worst and best our systems had to offer. I saw discrimination, fear, trauma, and hopelessness. Most of all, I had the pleasure of working with a remarkable woman in the midst of an uncontrolled whirlwind, that neither she nor I had any hope of stopping. I hope everyone finds a case such as this.

Meeting Faith

Faith Harper was a 37-year-old African female married to a 42-year-old Caucasian American male. The couple had been married for 20 years when she first entered our domestic violence shelter. I met Faith when she arrived at the domestic violence shelter for the first time. A psychologist at an inpatient psychiatric hospital referred her to the shelter. Faith's husband, Bob, petitioned to have her admitted to the psychiatric ward claiming that she was "unstable."

During our first meeting, Faith provided little personal information. It looked as if I would have to work with her awhile before learning a lot about her life. I wondered whether her culture affected the amount of personal information she would share with a Caucasian social worker. As in any professional relationship, I needed to build rapport before pushing her to provide the details of her life to a total stranger.

Yet, even in her reticence, Faith touched me in a way that no other client had done in the past. It was her style, I think. She was a woman of deference. That is, Faith maintained an air of politeness and a striking sense of personal pride, something I had not seen before. She treated everyone with respect, especially the children. She loved the children at the shelter. For a woman obviously in great personal turmoil, Faith still carried herself with purpose, as if she knew that she was capable.

Personal History

Faith came to the United States three years earlier from Kenya where she was a practicing general surgeon. She was a respected medical professional whom everyone admired. She gave up her medical practice to marry Bob. When asked why she gave up medicine and respect for marriage, Faith said that she assumed she could resume her medical career here. She did not know the difficulties in becoming a licensed physician in the United States, especially when she was not a citizen. Once she arrived, that dream essentially died. Faith occasionally worked odd-jobs at supermarkets or in hotels. One can only imagine the difficulties she had accepting workers' wages after being a respected medical professional in her country.

Marital History and Abuse

Faith met Bob when he visited Kenya on a business trip. They began dating in Kenya and continued their relationship over the Internet. She had also met another American man a couple of years earlier and they became engaged. However, after visiting him in the United States, they decided to call off the wedding. These were the only two personal relationships in Faith's life. She wanted to move to the United States, become a citizen, and live a better life. Despite her status in Kenya, the country was politically unstable and the economy poor. She believed that she would find happiness, success, and an excellent life if she lived in America. However, it did not seem as if anyone read her script.

Apparently, the Harper marriage was not blissful. Faith came to the shelter after revealing to her psychiatrist several occasions of domestic violence. She told the psychiatrist about years of beatings by her husband, and the psychiatrist determined it was domestic violence. As I would learn, Faith did not know the definition of domestic violence in the United States. In Kenya, domestic violence as a problem does not "exist." That is, men do beat their wives and abuse their children. It is simply not a crime. This was all "news" to her.

Right from the beginning of their marriage, Bob controlled her. He dictated whom she met, talked to, or befriended. He determined when she left the house, if at all. Quickly, Faith became Bob's property, to do with whatever he pleased. Next, he began demanding she participate in different sexual activities, including bondage and sadomasochism. Apparently, Bob had rape fantasies where he dominated Faith physically, mentally, and emotionally before raping her whenever he wanted. Once Bob established control, he began beating her. She reported that Bob beat, kicked, and choked her at least weekly. If she talked back or asked him to stop, Bob beat and raped her more often and with more anger.

When she began giving birth to children two years earlier, the rapes ceased. However, the beating, control, and public humiliations did not. Over time, Bob began telling his friends and family that Faith was "crazy." As time passed, nearly everyone that knew him, including neighbors, considered Faith mentally ill. People often expressed sympathy for Bob because his wife had so many problems. It was hard to determine the role that her Kenyan heritage, skin color, and speaking accent played in people's willingness to believe Bob's stories. Yet, given the history of racism and oppression in the United States (Johnson, 2004), it was easy to believe that these factors played an instrumental role in the believability of Bob's cover story. Meanwhile, and with nobody paying attention, Bob controlled her life and beat her whenever she spoke up, and sometimes when she did not speak at all.

Bob's strategy paid-off. Occasionally, Faith called the police after a beating. However, because she was "foreign" and "crazy," the police would not investigate. They usually asked Bob to stop her from calling, and to get Faith the help they believed she needed. Sometimes, the police did not even come to the house. Bob was able to pass off her injuries as accidents caused when she threw a tantrum. Clearly, Bob had created the "perfect" arrangement. He could beat, control, and rape his wife whenever he pleased. If she called out for help, people blamed it on her or refused to believe her because Faith was a "crazy African."

Faith also suspected that Bob was sexually abusing the children, especially their two-year-old son. Faith claimed to have witnessed Bob abusing their son on many occasions. She stated that he made her watch him "love" their son as a "father should." She also claimed to have physical proof of the abuse. She had called Child Protective Services (CPS) numerous times about the abuse. However, CPS workers ruled that her complaints were groundless and unsubstantiated.

Her First Day at the Shelter

When Faith arrived at the shelter, she was distraught. She was tearful and begging for help getting her children back. Bob had taken their two children (a 2-year-old boy and a 2-month-old girl) to his mother's home. At the time, Faith was breast-feeding their newborn and believed that her daughter would struggle adjusting to formula. Faith wanted her children back, but she did not want to return home. She was not working, had no driver's license, and no income. Bob recently lost his job because he could not get along with his co-workers.

While her case sounded serious, I wanted to know the sequence of events that led her to the shelter. Along with colleagues, I met with Faith for this purpose. Faith explained that she had made numerous complaints to Children's Protective Services

(CPS) in the county where she lived. She knew that Bob sexually abused her son, and suspected that his mother also was involved. One day earlier, Faith tried to stop Bob from taking the children to see their grandmother, but failed. He became violent, choked her, and forcefully took the toddler from her arms.

Later that day, a police officer arrived at her house with a petition for Faith's inpatient psychiatric committal. The police took Faith to the emergency room of the hospital in her area. A hospital social worker interviewed Faith about her current situation and her marriage. The social worker refused to admit her, and left to take a phone call. When the social worker returned, she insisted that Faith enter the inpatient psychiatric hospital for observation.

Faith questioned the social worker and asked why she believed hospitalization was necessary. The social worker told Faith that she spoke to Bob (the telephone call) and he told her a few things that made her believe psychiatric committal was in Faith's best interest. The social worker refused to reveal what Bob said about Faith. She was horrified that the social worker believed Bob, whom she had never met. Faith went to the inpatient psychiatric department of the same hospital where a psychiatrist completed another assessment. The psychiatrist said there was no reason for Faith to be involuntarily committed for psychiatric treatment. The doctor referred Faith to the shelter for help as a survivor of domestic violence. He believed that Faith was an abused woman needing a safe place to stay.

Faith told me that her husband filed the petition against her so he could take the children and render her stories unbelievable. While she spoke, Faith had a look of fear and pain on her face. She was frightened for her children, and herself. She pleaded for help.

As a staff, we were determined to help her in any way possible. We believed that we could make a difference in her life and told her so. Faith was mainly concerned about her children's safety and wanted to know if we could help her get her children back. We told Faith that we needed to make some telephone calls and learn more about the situation, but that we would do everything possible to help. Faith went to her room while staff members called our legal representative and the acting Shelter Director.

Questions

While domestic violence is common in practice, the authors hint that this is an unusual case. However, at this point in the case, beyond Faith's ethnic and racial background, it is similar to what you might find in any domestic crisis shelter in the United States. Therefore, before moving on, answer the following questions before moving ahead with this case.

1. What is your first hunch regarding the presenting problem? Explore the practice literature and discuss this issue with other students.

2. What is the next direction of inquiry and assessment? Explore the practice literature to locate theories or models that apply to domestic violence.

Based on the approaches you find, what information would you need to collect to perform a comprehensive and/or multi-systemic assessment? (See Chapter 1.)

3. Are there any practical issues to consider in this case before "treatment" begins? Explain your ideas.

4. What personal strengths can you locate and name at this early juncture in treatment?

5. Since Faith was from Kenya and married her husband after a short, long-distance Internet courtship, what cultural factors might play an important role in this case going forward?

Legal Issues: Child Custody and Ex Parte Orders

The staff met to discuss Faith's options. We contacted an attorney, who represented and advised many shelter clients, to meet with Faith. She advised Faith to file an ex parte child custody order for her children. When one party cannot attend legal proceedings for some reason, an ex parte order allows judges to make temporary decisions about child custody before scheduling a hearing where both parties are present. In our county, judges usually grant temporary child custody to the first person filing an ex parte order. Custody lasts at least until the formal custody hearing.

Faith filed her ex parte order first, and the judge granted her temporary child custody. The next step was to discover where Bob took the children. Faith believed that he probably took the children to his mother's house approximately 85 miles away. The acting Shelter Director's primary concern was about what might happen when we found the children. Our director wanted to ensure that we minimized any confrontation with Bob so that everyone remained safe. She did not want the kids caught in the middle of an aggressive encounter. With the help of the acting Director and other members of the staff, we developed a plan.

The attorney, two staff members, Faith, and I would pick up the children, enforcing Faith's custody rights under the ex parte order. They wanted to go to Faith and Bob's home first to be sure that the kids were not there before driving to the other house. We contacted the local police department and requested that they be ready to meet us at the house to make the transition as non-combative as possible. Staff members packed food, bottles, diapers, and car seats for the children. When we arrived at the house, we found Bob, the children, and the police. The police officers explained the ex parte order to Bob, and he complied by returning the children to Faith.

Faith and her children slept safely at the shelter that evening. The staff felt victorious in this case, and Faith was ecstatic. Faith had her kids back and could settle in and work toward creating a new life, away from Bob and the horrific violence he perpetrated against Faith and their son. She was adamant about not returning home because she feared for everyone's safety. We thought we had achieved her goal!

A New Court Order

The happiness did not last. Three days later, Bob served Faith with a court order forcing her to return the children to him. Bob retained an attorney to challenge the ex parte child custody order. Bob, through his attorney, stated that because Faith was from Africa, she was a flight risk. They argued that Faith would flee the country with the children. Although the children did not have passports and Faith did not have the money for airline tickets, the judge issued the order forcing her to return her children to Bob.

The news devastated Faith. She could not understand why a judge would allow such an order when she had no means to flee or family or friends in the United States to help her return to Africa. At the shelter, we were stunned. This was the first in a long line of incidents that shook our confidence about our ability to help Faith.

The next day, Faith decided to return home with her children. She believed that she should reconcile with Bob so she could monitor the children's well-being. She worried that Bob would sexually abuse the kids. Although Faith wanted a divorce, she decided to protect the children before worrying about her own desires. During one of our meetings, Faith told me that she felt unsafe at home. Based on her history with Bob, I could not blame her.

We worked on developing a safety plan. With Faith headed, by choice, back into the home where she suffered significant abuse, I thought it necessary for her to plan her inevitable escape. A safety plan entails encouraging clients to have an overnight bag packed and ready to go at all times (Davies, Lyon, & Monti, 1998). Faith decided to put clothes, nonperishable food, and items for the children in case she could take them with her. I also encouraged her to make overnight plans. That is, Faith needed to arrange a warm and safe place to spend the night. Faith agreed that she would do this as soon as Bob left for work. Faith's major problem was that she had no driver's license or money.

When she left the shelter, I worried about Bob beating her again.

Questions

Faith decided to return to an abusive man before allowing her children to leave without her. In domestic violence cases women often return to abusive partners, despite efforts by practitioners. However, this case appears different. There are many issues for practitioners to consider in Faith's case, including domestic violence, child sexual abuse, her "reputation" in the community, cultural factors, and potential racism and discrimination. Assume you are the practitioner responsible for this case when responding to the following questions.

1. **Explore the professional literature on cultural competence and human diversity to learn as much as possible about Faith's background and belief systems. Further, look for any empirical evidence or case reports about the affect of race, culture, and citizenship on child custody proceedings and/or CPS cases.**

2. **Based on your research, write an assessment of the structural and institutional factors that play a role in this case. Engage classmates and your instructor in a dialogue about these issues and their affect on practice.**

3. **Investigate the legal issues involving child custody in your state. If Faith lived in your state, how would her circumstances have changed, if at all? What factor must you know to be an effective practitioner/advocate for clients such as Faith in your locale?**

4. **Now that Faith decided to return to her marriage, what are your responsibilities as her practitioner? Examine the code of professional ethics to determine your approach, assuming that you can do anything at all.**

5. **What new hunches or ideas do you have about Faith's case? If you met her, what direction would you pursue to help her situation?**

6. **What specific plans would you implement to help Faith overcome her abusive situation?**

Faith Returns

We did not hear from Faith for one month. Then, suddenly, she was back in our lives. The police brought Faith to the shelter because Child Protective Services (CPS) had removed the children. While I was sad about the events, I was glad to see that she survived the previous month. However, this time Faith seemed more desperate and frustrated than the first time she was at the shelter. We struggled, similar to the first time, to understand the chain of events that led her to the shelter without her children.

We began by asking Faith to explain the events of the last month. Faith said that she could not stay at home any longer because she feared for her life. She was sure that Bob was planning to kill her. The longer she remained in the home, the stronger grew her belief that Bob was plotting her murder. The day before returning to the shelter, Faith packed up her children in the middle of the night, pushing them in a stroller to the only place she could find that looked safe. Later as she re-told this story to me, she shared that while walking away that night she felt calm, as if God approved of her leaving. She did not know where she was going only that she had to stay away from the routes Bob would drive to find her. Faith stopped at a campground with a chapel. The chapel was unlocked and had the essentials for Faith and her children to spend the night. There were blankets for everyone. They spent the night sleeping in the chapel.

When morning arrived, Faith went outside to find a telephone or someone to drive her to the shelter. Faith flagged down a jogger and explained that she needed a ride to the shelter to hide from her abusive husband. The jogger said she would be back to help. The police arrived about ten minutes later. It appeared that the jogger called the police to help her.

When the police arrived, Faith took her son outside to speak with the officers, leaving her daughter alone inside, strapped into her stroller. The officers recognized Faith, and knew of her family's history. Following a brief discussion, the police transported Faith to the police station and called CPS. After a brief discussion, the social worker from CPS claimed that Faith was neglectful for leaving her baby unattended in the chapel while she spoke with the police.

The temperature that night was 37 degrees. The CPS social worker claimed that Faith endangered her children by taking them outside in cold weather. According to Faith, both children were dressed in winter clothes, including outerwear. She also covered the baby with a heavy blanket. Faith said that her children were not in obvious distress and neither the police nor CPS thought that her children needed medical attention. Further, Faith said that during this process, nobody, not the police or CPS, asked her about why she left with the children. Officials did not seem interested in hearing Faith's stories about Bob's abuse and her fear that he would kill her. Of course, they already believed that Faith was crazy.

Within minutes, CPS removed the children from Faith's custody and sent them to a children's home in the area. Faith begged us to advocate for the children to stay at the children's home instead of returning them to Bob. However, the following day the kids were remanded to Bob's custody. The judge only permitted supervised visitations between Faith and her children.

Supervised Visits

The acting Shelter Director worked with the minister from Faith's church to determine a visitation schedule. They set visitation for Wednesdays from 9:00 a.m. to 3:00 p.m. at the shelter with our staff as supervisors. I waited in the office with Faith as her children arrived for their first supervised visit. Her son clung to her and laid his head on her shoulder. Faith had tears running down her face. Her simultaneous pain and relief were evident to everyone that day. When I witnessed the reunion, I believed that the children needed her. Hence, I needed to do everything possible, within the bounds of the code of professional ethics (NASW, 2000) to help her get them back. I would supervise their next three arranged visitations.

The judge scheduled a preliminary hearing regarding the CPS case four months hence. That meant Faith would be without her children while CPS investigated her case. Visitations continued, but did not go smoothly. On several occasions, Faith asked me to observe her children. Frequently, the children arrived for visits dirty, often in urine-stained clothing. Her son appeared to have rotten teeth and gums. It pained him to eat. During one visit, Faith learned that his teeth had broken off. His mouth looked painful and I took pictures to document their care. Bob obviously neglected the children, or was incapable of handling the responsibility. Either way, the kids were in bad shape. Faith was heartbroken and angry that nobody believed her. We did.

Our acting Director contacted CPS in hopes that they would come see the poor condition of the children. We believed that CPS would take Faith's stories seriously when they knew that we witnessed their inappropriate treatment. In our minds, now CPS had proof of Bob's neglect. They no longer had to worry about an angry Faith making false claims against her husband. We were ready and willing to verify their poor physical condition.

However, CPS did not respond. The social worker refused to come to the shelter, essentially telling us that we were mistaken. The CPS social worker seemed unconcerned and made little attempt to get Faith's son to a dentist. Remember, Faith was a surgeon in Kenya and knew what medical attention her children needed. Her knowledge and willingness to advocate for her children intimidated CPS more than impressed them. The CPS social worker decided that Faith was not a worthy doctor.

Questions

1. **Investigate the child protection process in your local state and county. If you were the practitioner in this case, what recourse would you have if you believed that a CPS worker was negligent?**

2. **What would you recommend the practitioner do with this case?**

3. **Can you think of any possible issues that might lead the CPS worker to act as if she/he was uninterested in Faith's story?**

Faith Recognizes Her Abuse

I spent a lot of time with Faith during her first few months at the shelter. Faith spent this time writing the history of her marriage. She wrote about the suspected sexual abuse against her children and about the abuse she endured at the hands of her husband. As Faith learned about domestic violence, she wrote about the details of her victimization. She also obtained copies of pertinent records of every event that occurred. She had all the medical files, all the documentation from CPS, and any other information she thought might be helpful in getting her children back.

Getting her children back became Faith's obsession. She wanted to prove to CPS and the judge that she had been telling the truth. She wanted them to believe the horrors she experienced with Bob. I encouraged her to write about everything that went on. I asked this for two reasons. First, this information might prove helpful in court. Second, I believed that journalizing her experiences might prove therapeutic.

Faith spent nearly all of her time researching and documenting her abusive marriage and concerns for her children. She compiled so much information that her legal representatives could not take the time to sort through Faith's records. What she intended as a helpful tool became a burden because of the amount of material. It did not help that her court-appointed attorney seemed disinterested in her case. Faith told me that her attorney fell asleep during one of their meetings. Faith began realizing that she might have to fend for herself.

Cultural Issues and Misunderstandings

I tried to help Faith understand how the system worked in the United States. She could not grasp the difference between U.S. culture and her native Kenyan culture. At home, she never knew discrimination. In Kenya, Faith was a respected professional woman; smart, successful, and social. In the United States, she was simply an African woman-of-color considered crazy by many and in trouble with CPS. The system did not see her intelligence but rather seemed to focus on her skin color, accent, and her community reputation. Unfortunately, Bob was a Caucasian American male. Little of this made sense to Faith. She was unaccustomed to being someone's chattel.

The time I spent with Faith was enlightening. I studied cultural competency in school, but never had the challenge of working with someone so different and with so many barriers to overcome to receive services. My education in real world social work practice had begun. I quickly learned not to believe everything you read in diversity textbooks. For example, I learned in school that African women dressed in bright colors. Faith came to the shelter with no clothes and refused to take anything from home. Faith considered anything from that home as evil and she was better off without them. I took her to a used clothing store the shelter operated for clients and the community. I helped her choose clothing and shoes. I suggested vibrant colors and prints. She laughed at me, saying that she preferred neutral colors and styles. That moment I learned to ask her about her beliefs and not assume I already knew them because I attended graduate school in social work.

Faith had a "proper" way about her, always conducting herself humbly with others. She was a private person as well, not talking openly about family or her childhood in her country. She laughed boisterously, making staff wonder if she was mentally ill, perhaps manic. Maybe she was simply an emotional African woman, or maybe that was simply her style. As she later told me, in her culture laughing aloud was acceptable and common. Yet, based on the reaction of our staff to her laughter, I began understanding how Bob could convince people that she was mentally ill. Her way was different, and that sometimes threatens people. In search for understanding, sometimes cultural misunderstanding is labeled as mental illness. Maybe this is what happened to Faith.

I found myself frustrated with CPS, the police, and the courts. CPS was not investigating her stories about Bob abusing her and the children. Instead, CPS was investigating Faith. I wondered if this occurred because she was not a U.S. citizen. I also continued to wonder how her race and interracial/intercultural marriage affected her situation (Moore, 1998). It seemed that she encountered discrimination at every turn. However, discrimination is difficult to prove. I was unsure what to do about her situation.

Faith and I talked about discrimination. She needed help and begged anyone and everyone to listen to her story. I said that while I did not know what to do, I would not stop asking questions until I learned what to do. While I may not find answers, I promised to keep trying. I remember how I felt that day driving home from the shelter, knowing that I had to find a way to help Faith. Faith needed an advocate before it was too late.

Taking Action and "Facing the Music"

I contacted a former co-worker to discover how I could advocate for Faith. He was an African American social worker with the experience I lacked in these matters. He suggested that I contact the NAACP, The Urban League, and the American Civil Liberties Union (ACLU). He said that these organizations would be a good place to start. Perhaps one of these organizations could help with legal resources and/or address the potential discrimination. I located print material about each organization so Faith could review them herself. I wanted to provide Faith the means to advocate for herself; to empower her to make decisions regarding her advocacy. Faith was happy. Perhaps one of these organizations could intervene on her behalf to help get her story out, and her children returned.

My supervisor did not appreciate my efforts to help Faith advocate for herself. My supervisor reprimanded me for my efforts. She called me into her office and told me that I overstepped my boundaries in the agency. My supervisor said that I did not have the authority to provide Faith with this information. Moreover, she complained that Faith would want her to visit all of the places and she did not have that much time to spend on her case. She reprimanded me for "making more work" for her. I was shocked. I believe that advocating on behalf of clients was my job as a social worker. I hoped that our agency was not giving up on Faith too.

I agreed with my supervisor that I should not overstep my authority. However, Faith deserved and needed the information and someone to advocate for her. Faith did not realize that organizations existed that could help her. While I agreed not to overstep my role again, I restated my concern that Faith needed extra effort, regardless of its affect on the agency and my supervisor's schedule. She then removed me from working with Faith. Others in the agency would handle her case.

Faith did not understand this move, and I did not go into details with her. I began wondering if the whole system was stacked against her. Even our agency, one built to protect and advocate for abused women and children, hesitated to take the "extra mile." As someone relatively new to social work, I was discouraged by how "helpers" treated this woman.

Because of the medical complaints registered by our staff, CPS moved the location of Faith's visits to their offices across town. A CPS worker would supervise her visits from then on. The CPS social worker said that she believed that our complaints were unjust and a "nuisance." Therefore, she punished Faith by moving her visits to an inconvenient location. CPS also reduced her visitation from six hours per week to two hours per week. Additionally, Faith could not feed, diaper, or wipe her children's noses. The CPS worker claimed that Faith medically examined the children and had traumatized them with the alleged examinations. Not only did CPS remove her children but also her right to parent and care for them. Again, Faith turned to the agency and me for help.

The acting Director kept telling her she needed to comply with CPS if she wanted a chance to get her kids back. This advice was the only help she received from the shelter on that matter. Each time something happened, Faith lost a little more hope. She came to the shelter with new found hope that we could help. She slowly lost her hope, replacing it with mistrust of a system that was abandoning her and her children.

Questions

It seems that Faith had little support in her efforts to gain custody of her children. Even the shelter, spearheaded by the acting Director, seemed to stop helping. Moreover, because the custody issue was so important to her, Faith stopped making progress in her treatment as a domestic violence survivor. Moreover, the acting Director reprimanded one of the authors for advocating for Faith by finding outside help for her legal problems.

Additionally, the authors have presented significant personal, familial, and multi-systemic information about Faith's situation. Therefore, assuming that you are the practitioner handling Faith's case, please respond to the following questions.

1. Based on the information provided, construct a three-generation genogram and eco-map that represents Faith's personal, familial, and environmental circumstances. What further information do you need to complete this exercise? What patterns do these two important graphical assessment tools demonstrate?

2. Compile a list of Faith's issues and strengths, drawing from multi-systemic sources.

3. Write a two- to three-page narrative assessment that encompasses Faith's multi-systemic issues and strengths. Review Chapter 1 if needed.

4. What is your professional opinion of the author's attempts to locate outside help? Compile two arguments for this question. First, construct an argument that supports the author's efforts. Second, construct an argument that supports the acting Director's position. Engage in a dialogue with classmates, with one group taking the author's position and another group taking the acting Director's position.

5. Consult the code of professional ethics (NASW, 2000) for guidance on this issue. What does the code say about the author's efforts?

The Acting Director Leaves: New Hope

The regular Shelter Director (Sue) returned from an extended medical leave, replacing the acting Director. The acting Director became the barrier to helping Faith in the previous few months. I suppose she acted conservatively in her temporary position. When Sue returned, Faith had been living at the shelter for three months. The time limit was usually six weeks. By this time, the staff felt unable to help her anymore. Sue spent time listening to Faith. She contacted people in the community to advocate for Faith. She spent several days working with Faith trying to develop a case for the return of her children.

First, Sue wanted to ensure that Faith grasped her domestic violence experiences. Sue and I explained the domestic violence power and control wheel. We wanted Faith to understand her relationship with her husband. As time passed, Faith demonstrated a better understanding of domestic violence in general, and specifically regarding her abuse by her husband. Faith recognized elements of her relationship in each section of the wheel and gained a better understanding about domestic violence. Faith began recognizing that she was a survivor of domestic violence, setting in motion the prerequisite for empowerment. That is, as she recognized her situation, Faith began changing in ways that reduced her chances of living in another abusive relationship. She became assertive and demanded a better life for her family. She expressed no desire to return to Bob. While Faith worried about finding another abusive man, she figured that this time she would work on her career and independence before beginning relationships with men.

Sue and I also met with the CPS worker to understand their position and to help with visitation. The Director supervised visitations herself to make sure that Faith was doing what CPS expected of her. Faith's confusion about CPS and the worker's attitude became the most difficult issue to overcome. Faith simply could not understand why nobody believed her stories. Faith also struggled to understand why she could no longer touch her children or change their diapers. Sue did the best she could to explain CPS policy to Faith, but to no avail. CPS did not help the situation.

As time passed, even the worker contradicted herself. For example, during one visit Faith's baby had diarrhea. Following CPS policy, Faith had to leave her child in his feces for the duration of the visit. At the conclusion of the visit, the CPS worker reprimanded Faith for not changing the diaper, despite the guidelines set by her organization. The CPS worker said that Faith should have taken care of her child. Sue took the worker aside and expressed her frustration. Yet, our frustration was nothing compared to Faith's frustration. She continued losing hope and her frustration slowly turned to anger. She became angry at the system, Bob, and sometimes staff at the shelter.

Faith Loses Faith

Faith began turning her anger toward the shelter and its staff. With each disappointment, Faith grew increasingly uncooperative around the shelter. She refused even the simplest suggestions. She was tired of the "American" system and wanted to return to Kenya. I worked with Faith individually, allowing her to cry and vent her feelings. Faith was fixated on going to court, getting her kids back, and leaving for Kenya. I found it impossible to blame her. We all watched as CPS and the legal system destroyed her and her children. It was painful to witness.

Faith stopped attending group counseling, a requirement for all residents at the shelter. She also refused participation in any planned activities. She filed a petition for a Personal Protection Order (PPO) against Bob and did not tell the staff until she was ready to leave for the hearing. She developed a file and had it delivered to the judge. Faith also fired her court-appointed attorney because he fell asleep during a meeting and disregarded her case.

Questions

According to the author's description, Faith became difficult to handle in the clinic settings.

1. What is your assessment of her situation?

2. Specifically, what interventions would you employ to help with the situation? Explain your ideas.

3. If you were the Director of the shelter, what would your response be to this situation?

Faith Goes to Court—Alone

I attended the PPO hearing and expected to see it dismissed. The judge was upset that Faith filed without legal counsel but proceeded with the hearing anyway. Bob sat with his attorney at the hearing and Faith sat by herself in front of the judge. She was stoic and confident, yet shed a few tears during the hearing. Initially, the judge reprimanded Faith for sending him a handwritten file. Faith told the judge that her court-appointed attorney was incompetent and that she had fired him. The judge decided to address that issue later.

He asked several questions about her reasons for wanting a PPO. She told the judge that Bob had choked her twice. Upon hearing this accusation, the judge asked for proof of her allegations. Faith quickly produced a document that Bob's attorney had previously filed in court that corroborated Faith's recollection of the domestic violence. Faith's ability to produce this document surprised the defense. The document verified that Bob had indeed choked Faith. When the judge questioned Bob about why he resorted to physical violence, he said he just couldn't "take it" anymore and could not stop himself.

The judge granted the PPO and told Bob that no matter what happened in the marriage, it was unacceptable to physically threaten or assault Faith in any way. He also admonished Bob that he should learn to manage his anger and should never harm anyone. He appeared angry at Bob's violent tendencies. The judge told Bob to learn to "walk off" his anger, not take it out on his wife, or anyone else.

After the successful hearing, we were jubilant! Faith had won the PPO hearing by proving that she was telling the truth, Bob had been an abusive husband. Outside the shelter, the judge was the first person to believe her. We now believed that Faith had provided the evidence required to have custody restored. This was a dream. While Faith had a PPO, the news did not change CPS. The worker still treated Faith as if she was a criminal. In our opinion, the CPS social worker did not want Faith to have custody of her children. She was not about to allow court testimony and proof of domestic violence stand in the way of her desired disposition of this case.

Preparing for the Custody Hearing

After the PPO hearing, I focused on helping Faith agree to accept legal counsel. We also believed that perhaps the judge was on her side. However, Faith refused my suggestion. She was going to do this her way. She closed off discussion about it. She said that she did not want our help anymore.

As part of the custody battle, Faith underwent a psychological evaluation. The process lasted six weeks. It included personality tests and standardized IQ tests. I was concerned that the tests might contain cultural biases that could hurt her case. Faith knew that she was at a disadvantage but agreed to take them. She wanted to convince the judge to return her children.

The bigger issue at this stage concerned Faith's behavior at the shelter. Faith refused to follow the shelter guidelines to seek a job, search for an apartment, and participate in counseling. Sue spoke to me about the need to discharge Faith from the shelter. It was not a decision made lightly or quickly. She made the decision because the shelter's funding sources required clients to participate in services and Faith was already beyond the four- to six-week time limit for a residential stay. After much discussion between Sue and me, we decided that I would confront Faith about her behavior in an effort to get her to participate. If she participated, Sue would waive the length of stay limits.

Faith did not budge. She was strong willed and stubborn, tired of being ignored, and frustrated by the helping system. She was done listening to our advice and input. Since she left Kenya, Faith had so little control in her life that she needed a sense of power over something. Unfortunately, she chose participation at the shelter as her "battleground," risking her only place to live in the process. I believed that she was not going to give up her control, even if it meant discharge from the shelter. Faith decided that she needed a "break," and left the shelter for the weekend.

Faith called on Monday and spoke to Sue about returning to the shelter. The Director said that she could re-enter, but only if she agreed to follow the guidelines that all clients followed. Faith agreed and was re-admitted. Faith was required to attend the domestic violence support group and to meet with me once a week for crisis counseling. She was also required to work toward finding employment and to seek independent housing once she secured an appropriate income. It was good to have her back.

Questions

As the case progresses, the authors present a lot of information describing their professional relationship with Faith. They also discuss the shelter's professional relationship with Faith. Some practitioners and instructors might say that the shelter and staff have crossed the boundaries of professionalism. Others, including the authors, would say that the shelter and staff provided for Faith in a way that met her needs. Based on the professional literature and your experience, what is your opinion of the professionalism and relationships forged with Faith? Explain your position.

Court Proceedings

The first court date finalized Faith's divorce from Bob. This made her happy, and represented a significant step away from living with domestic violence. Faith arrived at the shelter in April. She lived in the shelter six months. It had been five months since CPS removed her children. Faith was more than a little bit impatient.

The judge decided to continue the custody hearing two weeks later. When the hearing convened, the psychologist testified about the results of her evaluations of Bob and Faith. She diagnosed both Faith and Bob with Obsessive Compulsive Disorder (OCD). The psychologist also said that Bob had significant anger problems. The psychologist testified that the children needed time with their mother. Her absence and inability to function as their mother was traumatic for the children.

This court appearance was hard for Faith, but she believed that she would find justice in this courtroom. Faith took the witness stand and talked about Bob's abuse and troublesome sexual acts he forced on her. Faith testified in a clear, concise, and dignified manner, not once losing her temper or appearing disconnected. Her presence gave her credibility.

The judge delayed his decision, instead setting a third court date for two months hence. In the interim, CPS increased Faith's visitation time from two hours per week to four hours per week. While her case appeared to be moving in her favor, Faith was about to suffer one more shocking twist in her life.

HIV/AIDS

For several weeks, Faith had not been feeling well. Finally, she wanted to see a doctor. Since Faith was a physician, she knew something was wrong. Faith told me about her swollen glands and fever. She feared that she was seriously ill, perhaps cancer.

One week later, Faith visited the doctor. Her physician performed a series of blood tests, including a test for HIV. He returned a diagnosis of HIV. Faith was HIV positive, and her blood work suggested that her condition would soon become full-blown AIDS. What more could happen to this woman? I wondered how she contracted this disease. Her only two lifetime sexual partners were Bob and the man she visited in the United States a few years earlier. She said they only had sexual intercourse once. That left Bob. What about the children? I wondered when she contracted HIV. Of course, with the HIV/AIDS epidemic in the continent of Africa, perhaps she had the disease before coming to the United States.

Faith's responded by withdrawing from everyone, including Sue and me. She did not want to tell me, because she did not want to "hurt" me. Obviously, I had become too close to Faith. She no longer considered me a social worker, but a friend. Faith finally decided to talk with Sue and local public health workers. The health department needed to test Bob and the children too. Surprisingly, Bob tested negative while both of the kids tested positive. Furthermore, the strain of HIV she contracted was from the United States. Faith did not contract the disease in Kenya, but in United States. Her former fiancé must have given her HIV a few years earlier.

My heart dropped when I heard this news. Beyond worrying about her health, I wondered what this revelation would do to her custody case. Would she ever get her kids back? What judge would give kids to a mom with AIDS? I worried even more about the children. Both had HIV.

Because of her medical background, Faith knew universal precautions better than everyone did. She operated in a way that kept others safe. She wore latex gloves whenever she did chores around the shelter. CPS switched visitation sites back to the shelter. Her HIV status created new issues for worker and client safety. Both children were sick but the baby was the sickest; she had full-blown AIDS.

One day Faith left the shelter for a visit. She failed to tell anyone where she had gone, and staff worried. The Board of Directors, over Sue's vehement argument, decided to discharge Faith. They decided that her case had gotten too big for the shelter to handle. Moreover, they became worried about the effect Faith's presence in the shelter might have on their future funding. Since much of their funding came from private donors in a politically conservative community, they worried that donors would cease supporting the shelter if they knew Faith had HIV/AIDS.

After discharge, I helped Faith find a subsidized apartment. Despite her failing health, Faith continued visiting her children at CPS. This was one more blow to her life, and one more hurdle to overcome. As always, Faith handled it with grace and aplomb.

Questions

This case makes you wonder how much a person can handle, huh? Regardless, as helping professionals her HIV/AIDS diagnosis presented several issues to consider. Explore the professional literature and best practice evidence to answer the following questions.

1. What does her diagnosis mean for treatment? That is, what new approach or interventions are needed to address Faith's problems?

2. What medical arrangements must happen to ensure that Faith receives the help she needs?

3. Explore the available resources for poor women with HIV/AIDS in your state. What resources would Faith need to address her life at this point?

4. What is your opinion about the shelter's decision to discharge Faith? Weigh the options as if you were the director. How would you balance Faith's needs versus the community's? Based on your assessment of the situation, what decision would you make about Faith and her ability to remain at the shelter?

Final Disposition

Her final custody hearing occurred in June. Again, the judge decided to delay his decision until October. In October, the judge denied Faith custody of her children, leaving permanent visitation up to CPS. Faith did not attend the final hearing. Her attorney mailed Faith a letter to tell her about the decision. The lawyer did not want to deal with Faith's reaction to the decision.

Epilogue

Faith drifted away after the hearing. I heard that she entered a residential home for AIDS sufferers in a distant city. Both children died within two years of the hearing. I am sure that Faith also passed, but I do not know this for sure. Perhaps she found a way to afford the new antiretroviral drugs that essentially save HIV/AIDS sufferers from an early death.

While I have long since left the shelter, I still think about Faith. I tell her story every chance I get. Clearly, everyone victimized Faith, including the system and our shelter. I share her story in hopes that this will never happen again. I want society to become more aware about domestic violence and the gender, racial, and institutionalized discrimination that exist in our social service and legal systems.

This was a story about a woman who fell in love with a man and moved to his country to marry him. Her husband abused her and the system abused her even more. Remarkably, Faith learned about abuse, and knew what happened to her. Had she remained healthy, I have no doubt that she would have found happiness in a life that did not include abusive and controlling male partners.

Faith's case also demonstrates the power of culture and the need for cultural competence across the social service system. Although she was highly educated and professional, she did not understand American culture and the social service and legal systems. Unfortunately, Bob did, and he used the system against her. Moreover, I believe people working in the system (shelter, CPS, and the courts) also used her lack of knowledge and cultural differences against her, even if they were not consciously aware of it. To American social workers, Faith's normal cultural expressions looked like mental illness. Hence, everyone treated her as such. I also believe that her diagnosis of OCD lacked credibility, given the cultural biases embedded in the psychological evaluation process (Moore, 1998).

In the end, who knows what was real in her case. Unfortunately, only one person did, and nobody believed her.

Questions

The authors presented an interesting and difficult domestic violence case. As is most often true, this case involved many problems and issues beyond the presenting complaint. Taking a broad view of this case, reevaluate the author's work and your participation through the questions asked throughout the case.

1. Take a moment to review Faith's progress. Based on the author's description, the professional literature, and the latest practice evidence, what occurred to account for her progress?

2. What was the theoretical approach or combination of approaches that appeared to work best for Faith?

3. Based on the work you have done earlier, what additional intervention(s) would you recommend? Use the literature and latest evidence to justify your recommendations.

4. Overall, what is your professional opinion of the work performed in this case? As always, refer to the professional literature, practice evidence, your experience, and the experience of classmates when developing your opinion.

5. Evaluate the authors' claims about the social service systems in this case. Based on your reading and information gleaned through discussions and/or experience, respond to their opinion that faith was victimized by the system? The authors mentioned discrimination. Examine the literature to find the theoretical and legal definitions of discrimination. Did that occur in this case?

6. Evaluate the authors' work, specifically regarding their relationship with Faith. Given your experience and knowledge about professional relationships in practice, what is your opinion about their relationships with Faith in this

case? Does the code of ethics shed any light on this issue? Explain and justify your opinion.

7. What did this case demonstrate that you could use in other practice settings. List the most important things you learned from this case and how you could use them in your practice career.

Bibliography

Davies, J., Lyon, E., & Monti, C. D. (1998). *Safety planning with battered women: Complex lives/difficult choices.* Thousand Oaks, CA: Sage.

Johnson, J. L. (2004). *Fundamentals of substance abuse practice.* Pacific Grove, CA: Brooks/Cole.

Moore, R. B. (1998). Racism in the English language. In P. Rothenberg (Ed.), 4th ed. *Race, class, and gender in the United States* (pp. 465–475). New York: St. Martin's Press.

National Association of Social Workers. (2000). *Code of Ethics of the National Association of Social Workers.* Washington, DC: Author.